El Jazim

Say YES!

El Jazim

Say YES!

Albert Waszink

Winchester, UK
Washington, USA

JOHN HUNT PUBLISHING

First published by O-Books, 2023
O-Books is an imprint of John Hunt Publishing Ltd., 3 East St., Alresford,
Hampshire SO24 9EE, UK
office@jhpbooks.com
www.johnhuntpublishing.com
www.o-books.com

For distributor details and how to order please visit the 'Ordering' section on our website.

ISBN: 978 1 80341 016 6
978 1 80341 017 3 (ebook)
Library of Congress Control Number: 2021944039

A CIP catalogue record for this book is available from the British Library.

Design: Stuart Davies

UK: Printed and bound by CPI Group (UK) Ltd, Croydon, CR0 4YY
Printed in North America by CPI GPS partners

Contents

Foreword

Dear reader,

We are living in the end time. This doesn't mean the end of our planet. It is a time during which Earth is affected by a huge increase of Light Energy, and this increased Light Energy may allow you to turn from an ego-centred awareness to a heart-centred awareness.

I have written this book to help you achieve that. It outlines the whole concept in a broader perspective but it also explains the details of the transfer itself; what it means for you and what you can do to stimulate it.

The large influx of Light Energy is also making more and more people perceptible to make contact with highly developed souls who live outside the material worlds. And this leads to a lot of new information. Moreover, an increasing number of people are able to remember experiences locked away in their souls and this also provides fast-growing new insights. Thanks to the Internet, this information is now quickly available to nearly every person around the world. Even so, much of this information that is out there is jumbled and disorganised and, thus, lacking the broader perspective and making it hard to digest. Another factor is that people often parrot one another without having personal experiences themselves. All of this makes it hard for the novice religious or spiritual seeker to see the forest for the trees.

With this book, I hope to offer a vast amount of knowledge that was lost or kept hidden. I also add structure to that knowledge so that you will not just gain clearer insight into the broader perspective of the end time but also into the opportunities that this end time may offer you.

And lastly, this book was written to interconnect.

It interconnects Judaism, Christianity, and Islam by restoring their common foundations.

Furthermore, it shows the links between the exoteric teachings of Judaism, Christianity, and Islam and the esoteric teachings by explaining these esoteric teachings and their development stages to the wider public. These stages are based on the development stages that Jesus taught his disciples and as they are described in the Bible.

Besides that, it interconnects the developments taught by spiritual non-religious communities and the three mentioned religions.

Lastly, it links religion to development psychology and transpersonal psychology as the development stages that it describes match those experienced in transpersonal psychology and because the development pattern of every stage matches the development pattern taught in development psychology.

In short, my purpose for writing this book is to provide a manual for everyone who is interested in religion and also for everyone who is interested in spiritual development, regardless of having a religious, spiritual, or scientific background.

I have done my utmost to keep the book easy to read and practical. However, I have not always succeeded because there is one God and this one God is indivisible. As God is indivisible, God can never be contradictory. All is one. On the other hand, our intellect, our thinking ability, is fully based on antitheses, making it difficult for me to describe how I experience the oneness of God and, thus, hard for you to understand. Still, you can understand God, not through your intellect but from the heart.

This is why I address you, the reader, directly in this book. I do this to touch your heart.

Your intellect will probably, at some point, falter when trying to understand the words you are reading. When this happens, never hesitate and realise that the oneness of God is something that our intellect simply cannot understand. Just in case you are on the brink of giving up, I have added chapter 21 The Core Message. This chapter contains everything you need to know.

Go with God

1

The End Time

The age we live in today is called the 'end time'. It is the time as predicted by John in the Book of Revelation. That doesn't mean that Earth is on the cusp of extinction. It does mean that, right now, we are going through a time of significant changes. These changes are caused by four developments that are currently taking place at the same time and which will have far-reaching effects on how humanity and Earth continue to develop and exist. We are talking about the following occurrences:

1. There is an increasing influx of Light Energy with a higher frequency than before.
2. The soul of Earth goes through new stages and needs to change.
3. A part of the human souls needs to move on to a next development stage.
4. Alien souls are born on Earth to help mankind.

1 There is an increasing influx of Light Energy with a higher frequency than before

In this day and age, the frequency of Light Energy that affects Earth is increasing. This applies to our entire solar system and all other star systems around us and these changes are cyclical. It is a fact that we have to deal with and which makes it easier for people to grow spiritually. It becomes easier to release ego-centred energies and attract heart-centred energies.

2 The soul of Earth goes through new stages and needs to change

Like any living creature, Earth has a soul, which is also named

Gaiael, or Gaia. When Gaiael was created, she felt the need to individualise and gain experiences. She wanted to create and, influenced by the Love Light that she attracted, Earth came into existence. Gaiael attracted energies that she then devoured. She consumed the energies and grew denser and denser. In some way, this energy consumption was a creative process as it led to the creation of Earth but, at the same time, it was a deadly process as the attracted energies were consumed. Gaiael didn't add anything to the energies, she just devoured them. No life existed on Earth, and Earth was a dead planet that only took but gave nothing.

After an endless amount of time, Gaiael slowly began to long for something new. She wanted to create instead of just destroy, to give instead of take, and in her longing for something new, she attracted new energies. Helped by the archangels, who will be discussed later on, Gaiael slowly grew to become an environment suitable for receiving life. The Earth crust cooled, land and oceans were formed, as well as an atmosphere. At first, the atmosphere was very wild, with violent winds and huge thunderstorms discharging of vast amounts of energy but, in time, the atmosphere quieted down.

Souls are born in waves and God created a new wave of souls. These new souls attached themselves to the most primitive lifeforms on Earth, the single-cell organisms. They are called Earth souls, the indigenous organisms that have Earth as their home base.

Life on Earth then developed according to Darwin's theory of evolution, although we should bear in mind that the development of life is not some biological coincidence but the development of the underlying quality of Earth souls, or of their consciousness. As Earth souls continued to develop, they needed more complex living beings through which they could express themselves and this resulted in the development of biological structures in which they gained experiences.

Gaiael was overjoyed that life was growing on her. Instead of taking, she could now start giving, and life on Earth continued as an entirely independent and creative process that formed all sorts of new lifeforms. Modern man came into existence when the evolution was ready to have us.

Today, mankind is taking more from Earth than Earth can give. Mankind is exhausting Earth, and Gaiael feels the limits of what she can give. She has had enough and is ready for a new development stage in which the balance of give and take will be restored. Life, as it exists on Earth now and which is draining it of its resources fast, can no longer continue as it does. Hence, changes will come that find their source through the increased consciousness of Gaiael.

3 A part of the human souls needs to move on to a next development stage

As life developed on Earth, modern man was formed at some point. The unique feature of modern man is that he has a will of his own. And he wants to use that will to exercise power and influence his environment. Being aware of one's individuality and using the will to exercise power for one's own benefit is called ego. Mankind has first discovered and developed his ego and experiences it to a very large extent. Furthermore, mankind has also experienced what will happen when you turn away from love and oneness and start to revel in egoism and lose yourself in negative emotions like fear, anger, and depression. All of this leads to battle, wars, loneliness, and suffering. A part of the human souls experienced this expression caused by the ego to the fullest and have now come to a point that they want to take another path. These people are looking for the oneness that calls out to them as a memory hidden away within their souls. They are looking for meaning in altruism and love for others, which they find in new age movements and spiritual development. Driven by love, they long to release the creativity of the Divine. They are ready to make the transfer from an ego-centred awareness to a heart-centred awareness.

4 Alien souls are born on Earth to help mankind

When people discovered and developed their ego, and started to live by it, they also became susceptible to external influences that latched on to the ego. Souls of alien species took advantage of this by interfering with humans in a very advanced way, through genetic manipulation and technologies that affect a person's thoughts and emotions. They implemented emotions such as fear, obedience and insensitivity into the minds of people so they could turn into perfect armies of soldiers. As a result, people were no longer able to develop freely. These alien species did this because they were fighting battles amongst themselves. In some way, this fight was brought to Earth, where it raged on between the different peoples and tribes for a long time. By now, however, the alien species who were responsible for this have developed further. They have given up their fight and moved on from an ego-centred awareness to a heart-centred awareness. They are 'enlightened souls' who live in love and oneness.

Some of them wish to atone for their guilt and decided to be reborn as people on Earth. These people are the so-called new age, indigo, crystal, or rainbow children. They literally are star people, lightbringers and lightworkers, galactic warriors for light and love. There is absolutely no reason for anyone to fear these lightbringers. They have all our best interests at heart and are only here to bring light to the world and help those who are ready to be helped. These lightbringers often find it hard to get used to life on Earth. They can be recognised by the following character traits:

- They are hypersensitive (HSP).
- They feel different, excluded, and often feel lonely and

misunderstood.

- They don't care for authorities who wield power over them, and find it hard to conform to existing structures and social etiquette.
- As children, they are often wise beyond their years.
- They feel the need to help others and find work that allows them to do that.
- They don't feel at home on Earth and cannot handle dishonesty, selfishness, and aggression very well. They often have vague or even clear memories of the world of light they originate from.
- They care deeply for nature, animals, and the environment. Many of them are vegetarians.
- They may not feel properly grounded but can seem 'woolly' within their own inner world.
- They often lived previous lives on Earth during which they were involved in religion or spirituality.
- Many of them are still burdened by traumas from previous lives, during which they were ousted, killed, or declared insane. If they were women during these previous lives, they might have been burned as witches.

I estimate that, at this moment, there must be around 100 million lightbringers incarnated on Earth and I expect that another 100 million will be born over the next 10 to 15 years, bringing their number to a total of 200 million. I beseech everyone to empathise with these lightbringers as they are so challenged in life, to be grateful for the helping task that they are taking on, and to welcome them.

2

Abbadon and the Locusts

John the Apostle had visions about the end time and he wrote those visions down in the Book of Revelation. People who read the Book of Revelation may become frightened as it seems apocalyptic and predicts terrible disasters but this should not be interpreted literally. That is why I would like to explain the meaning of chapter 9 of the Book of Revelation. First, I will quote to you what it says:

> [1]*The fifth angel sounded his trumpet, and I saw a star that had fallen from the sky to the earth. And the star was given the key to the shaft of the Abyss.* [2]*When he opened the Abyss, smoke rose from it like the smoke from a gigantic furnace. The sun and sky were darkened by the smoke from the Abyss.* [3]*And out of the smoke locusts came down on the earth and were given power like that of scorpions of the earth.* [4]*They were told not to harm the grass of the earth or any plant or tree, but only those people who did not have the seal of God on their foreheads.* [5]*They were not allowed to kill them but only to torture them for five months. And the agony they suffered was like that of the sting of a scorpion when it strikes.* [6]*During those days people will seek death but will not find it; they will long to die, but death will elude them.* [7]*The locusts looked like horses prepared for battle. On their heads they wore something like crowns of gold, and their faces resembled human faces;* [8]*their hair was like women's hair, and their teeth were like lions' teeth.* [9]*They had breastplates like breastplates of iron, and the sound of their wings was like the thundering of many horses and chariots rushing into battle.* [10]*They had tails with stingers, like scorpions, and in their tails they had power to torment people for five months.* [11]*They had as king over them the angel of the Abyss, whose name in*

Hebrew is Abaddon and in Greek is Apollyon (that is, Destroyer). [12]*The first woe is past; two other woes are yet to come.*

[13]*The sixth angel sounded his trumpet, and I heard a voice coming from the four horns of the golden altar that is before God.* [14]*It said to the sixth angel who had the trumpet, 'Release the four angels who are bound at the great river Euphrates.'* [15]*And the four angels who had been kept ready for this very hour and day and month and year were released to kill a third of mankind.* [16]*The number of the mounted troops was twice ten thousand times ten thousand. I heard their number.* [17]*The horses and riders I saw in my vision looked like this: Their breastplates were fiery red, dark blue, and yellow as sulphur. The heads of the horses resembled the heads of lions, and out of their mouths came fire, smoke and sulphur.* [18]*A third of mankind was killed by the three plagues of fire, smoke and sulphur that came out of their mouths.* [19]*The power of the horses was in their mouths and in their tails; for their tails were like snakes, having heads with which they inflict injury.*

[20]*The rest of mankind who were not killed by these plagues still did not repent of the work of their hands; they did not stop worshipping demons, and idols of gold, silver, bronze, stone and wood—idols that cannot see or hear or walk.* [21]*Nor did they repent of their murders, their magic arts, their sexual immorality or their thefts.*

(Book of Revelation 9:1-21)

The bottom line of what John says is that Abaddon, the angel of the abyss, will rise from the abyss together with the 200 million locusts he reigns over. The locusts will kill one-third of mankind and the two-thirds who stay alive will keep on worshipping the demons. So how to interpret all this?

Who is Abaddon and who are the locusts? The general consensus is that the name Abaddon means: 'Destroyer'. This assumption is incorrect. The name has an altogether different meaning and is also spelled incorrectly. The correct spelling is: 'Abbadon'. This name derives from the words 'Abba Don', meaning 'Father Lord' in Hebrew. The original name was 'Baba Don', which also means 'Father Lord'. This name, which actually was an honorary title, was the name of one of the kings who ruled over Atlantis. This king was the incarnation of one of the 24 Elders, the archangel Muriel. About Muriel, the following saga is known:

> *When God wanted to create man, he asked one of the archangels to fetch some clay so he could mould the first humans. The archangel, however, politely refused. God then asked the second archangel, and he also refused. And also, the third, the fourth, the fifth, and the sixth archangel refused to do God's bidding. Then God asked Muriel and Muriel fetched the clay from which God created man.*

The saga symbolises the creation of mankind and the first land they lived on. This land was founded by Muriel and named after him: 'Mu' or 'Lemuria'. Le-mu-ria derives from Mu-riel and means: Land of Muriel.

Around 4500 years ago, Muriel decided to be born in Egypt and become Pharaoh. He was born as the son of the pharaoh at the time and received his education in the temple where priests and pharaohs were trained. When he became of age, he had to go through the required initiations. He was brought inside the initiation pyramid where he had to scale a narrow staircase along a bottomless pit as his first test. But in this bottomless pit lived the Elementals who were charged to suck any person with just the tiniest ego-centred awareness into this pit. Muriel could feel the Elementals pulling and sucking, and he became frightened. He failed to pass the bottomless pit and didn't pass the test. The abyss that is mentioned in the Book of Revelation is this same bottomless pit and it has two meanings.

The first meaning is the actual bottomless pit inside the initiation pyramid. The second, symbolic meaning is the ego's search for satisfaction in external circumstances. The ego is a bottomless pit. The ego seeks satisfaction in external things but it will never find it. The ego gets lost in emotions such as fear, anger, depression, and suffering, and finds it nigh impossible to free itself from these emotions. The ego wields power but will ultimately end up drained and lonely. The ego is a bottomless pit of misery.

Muriel fell into the bottomless pit that is the ego, and he fell deep. But deep within this pit, Muriel looked death in the eye and accepted and conquered death, and emerged again as 'King of the bottomless pit'. What the story wants to convey is that he overcame his ego-centred awareness and transferred to a heart-centred awareness. The fifth trumpet sounded and Baba Don turns into Muriel again.

The name Muriel means 'Essence of God'. One important thing that should be noted is that the word 'essence' in English can also refer to scent, and this is why the unjustified conclusion was drawn that his name meant something like 'Perfume of God'. But Muriel doesn't mean Perfume of God at all. The Essence of God stands for Existence-Consciousness-Bliss. In Sanskrit, this is translated as: 'Sat-Chit-Ananda'. Nobody has to fear Muriel. He is not a destroyer, a devil, or someone who brings death. He is an archangel who has endured what all people endure: 'the experience of the ego-centred awareness', and he has overcome.

Locusts appear from the smoke rising up from the bottomless pit. Their number is twenty thousand times ten thousand, so 200 million. The outward appearance of the locusts is meticulously described and this shows that they are not literally locusts. They are creatures with the body of a horse and the face of a man. They are centaurs. The centaur represents the person who has overcome his ego-centred awareness and lives from the heart. The centaur symbolises the enlightened person who is firmly grounded but also spiritually enlightened. That is why centaurs are depicted wearing a golden crown.

The 200 million centaurs who rise up from the smoke in the bottomless pit of the ego are, in fact, the 200 million lightbringers who are now incarnating on Earth. They have come to help those of us who are ready to climb up from the pit of our egos as well. One-third of the people will die, meaning that they will die to their ego. They will transcend their ego-centred awareness and their heart-centred awareness will open up. These people are not the ones who should be lamented. On the contrary, they are the ones who will be elevated. They are the ones who will bear 'God's seal' on their forehead. Two-thirds of the population on Earth will not transcend the ego-centred awareness. They will continue to worship the demons of their ego.

The prophecies in the Book of Revelation were written down a very long time ago. And prophecies always lack a certain level of accuracy as the future offers countless paths and, thus, cannot be predicted. This is also why we cannot be absolutely sure that the number of lightbringers will be exactly 200 million, or whether the population who will transcend to a heart-centred awareness will be precisely one-third. However, we can state with certainty that we are now living in the prophesied end time and that this time offers wonderful opportunities to realise spiritual enlightenment.

Here is a message from Archangel Muriel to all the lightbringers who are now incarnated on Earth and to those who will incarnate on Earth. These are Muriel's own words:

Dear lightbringers,
On behalf of the 24 Elders of Earth and all Earth souls who yearn for light and love, I welcome you.

We are glad and rejoice in the fact that you have accepted the task to help us and open and enlighten our hearts.

Your task is not an easy one. You are often misunderstood and, sometimes, even shunned, but please know that you're not alone.

You may feel the urge to fight for the light, but you don't have to. You have fought long and hard enough. You don't have to 'do' anything, your presence is enough and crucial.

You are lightbringers, bringing light to Earth through your presence. And we thank you for that.

We hope and pray that your lives will be an example and beacon for us all and that your hearts will overflow with love.

Muriel

3

The First Name of God

In the next chapters, I will first restore the common foundations of Judaism, Christianity, and Islam, the core foundations that connect these three religions. Judaism, Christianity, and Islam are three branches of the same tree. They all grow from the same trunk. This trunk has a root and this root is the name of God.

Once a year, during the sacrificial ceremony of Yom Kippur, the high priest of the Jews entered the Holy of Holies where he atoned for all Jews and spoke the name of God. The latter Holy is the big temple in Jerusalem. The Holy of Holies is the little room in the centre of the temple. Only the high priest was allowed to enter this space. If you are Jewish, that is why the name of God is so important to you.

Christians pray: 'Our Father who art in heaven, hallowed be Thy name,' and they also baptise in the name of the Father and the Son and the Holy Spirit. If you are a Christian, that is why the name of God is so important to you.

The word Islam means 'submission'. Those people who submit to God are Muslims. So if you are a Muslim, the name of God, to whom you submit yourself, is important to you. In Islam the last name of God is unknown. Muslims are waiting for the person who will announce the last name of God, for they believe that this person will also announce the coming of the Messiah. For this reason the name of God is important for the Muslims.

The days that only the high priest was allowed to enter the Holy of Holies are long past. These days actually ended when Jesus died on the cross but this was not clearly conceived at the time. When Jesus died on the cross, the veil that separated the Holy of Holies from the rest of the temple ripped. The ripping of the veil was a sign that Jesus' death on the cross opened the path to the Holy of Holies. The death of Jesus symbolises the death of the ego. Jesus said that you first need to die before you can live. What these words of Jesus mean to say is that you die to your ego. You can die to your ego by opening your heart and submitting yourself to God, and you can live by speaking God's name in your heart, which is the Holy of Holies.

From now on, you may enter the Holy of Holies and speak the name of God. The latter Holy is your body. The Holy of Holies is your heart. It is your given right to speak the name of God in your own heart and to be hallowed by speaking his name.

So what is this name of God, that holy name that makes you whole and gives life when you speak it in your heart, this holy name that God revealed to Moses?

The name of God is 'El Jazim'.

The name of God consists of three elements: El, Ja, and Zim.

'El' means God; 'Ja' means 'yes'; and 'Zim' is the imperative of the verb 'to be'. So the name of God literally means: 'God-yes-be'.

In Judaism five names have derived from the name El Jazim.

The first name is: El.

The second name is: Eloah. This name derives from El Ja.

The third name is: Elohim. this name derives from El Oahim which derives from El Jazim.

The fourth name is: JHWH. This name derives from Jazim. The four-syllable word JHWH consist of two parts. The first part is Yah, which means 'yes' and the second part is Weh, a form of the verb 'to be'. The Jews assume that this is the form 'is' or 'am', but the correct form is the imperative 'be'.

The fifth name is: El Hasjeem. This means 'God the Name' as 'sjeem' means 'name'.

In Islam there are also two names derived from the name El Jazim.

The first name is: Allah. The name Allah is derived from El Ja, El Ja in Arabic is Al Ja. From Al Ja is the name Al-lah or Allah derived.

The second name is the 33rd name of God: Al Azim.

The meaning that Islam gives to the name Al Azim is 'the Great' or 'the Magnificent'. God is the greatest because he is the Creator. God creates the Creation by speaking the word Zim and he confirms the Creation by speaking the word Yes. The entire Creation originates from God and returns to God. God encompasses Creation and, therefore, there is nothing greater than God.

The name El Jazim means God saying Yes. It is God's Yes as He forms, confirms, and loves the entire Creation at any moment. 'Zim' forms Creation and 'Yes' confirms it. The word 'Yes' spoken by God is God's confirmation that Creation is perfect. All of Creation, every part of it, so you, too, are created perfectly to the image of God, and so God says Yes to every part of Creation, meaning also to you. 'Yes, I create you. Yes, you are good as you are. Yes, you are perfect as I am perfect in Heaven. You are my Creation. You are my Son. You are good as you are. Yes, I love you. Yes, I pour out my Love over you, at any moment of the day, as an unwavering blessing and mercy. My Love is embedded inside you, surrounds you, and fills you. My love is me saying Yes to you and the entire Creation.'

To hallow means 'to declare holy'. To hallow means 'to make as one'. God's name doesn't need to be hallowed. God's name, by itself, is already holy. You are hallowed by God's name. His name makes you as one. In his name, you are united with all of mankind and the entire Creation. His 'Yes' is your life. Yes is love. No is not love. If you say 'no' to someone, you reject that person. 'Yes' is not a rejection. 'Yes' accepts. 'Yes' never forsakes the works from his hands. The name of God is El Jazim.

Christians pray: 'Our Father who art in heaven, hallowed be Thy name.' But the name of God doesn't need to be hallowed.

The name of God is already holy as it is. Whoever speaks his name will be hallowed. Jesus taught his followers to pray: 'Our Father who art in heaven, we are hallowed by your name.'

God's name is more than an unconditional Yes from him to you. It confirms more than his unconditional love for you. It is also an invitation. God invites you to speak his name and thus claim your birthright. You can speak his name, and by speaking his name you will be hallowed.

Now take a moment of silence and pray, and when it feels right for you, then speak out God's name. Say Yes to God and love him above all else and love your neighbour as yourself. Say Yes to God and submit yourself completely to him. Say Yes to God so that his Love may radiate in your heart.

The name of God is El Jazim. As God says Yes to you, you are created and hallowed by his name. Praise God, Hallelu-jah!

4

The Last Name of God

Islam has many names for God although not all Islamic schools of theology agree on the exact number. Most Muslims accept that there are 99 known names for God, others believe there are 66 names. In order to know the last name of God, the exact number of names is not important. Important is the 33rd name of God. In numerology the highest number is 33. The 33rd name of God is El Jazim of which the name Al Azim is derived.

God is the alpha and the omega. He is the beginning and the end. He is the first and the last. All of Creation comes forth from God and ends in God. El Jazim is the first name of God and El Jazim is also the 33rd and last name of God.

Muslims already know that. Because the 33rd name Muslims have for God is Al Azim and the first name they have for God is Allah, which is actually the same as Al Azim, without the part 'Zim'.

As a cut diamond has different facets, God has many names. And every name of God tells something about God as every facet of a cut diamond says something about the diamond. Every name represents a feature of God. The diamond itself, God, also has a name. The name that God revealed to Moses is El Jazim, which means: God-yes-be, or God saying Yes. El Jazim is the name of God that encompasses all other names.

One can give many names to God, even more than 33. That has happened and there is nothing wrong with that. If somebody is in love with somebody else the lover thinks his beloved has the most beautiful features. God, my beloved, is the most beautiful, the sweetest, the only one, the greatest, the best, the magnificent. These are features that the devotee sees in God.

But no matter how many names God has, the 33rd is always

the last one, because 33 is the highest number. That's why El Jazim is the last name of God, even if God had a thousand names.

God can be honoured by giving him many beautiful names, but it is better to speak his name, fully conscious of its meaning. That's why I advise you: 'Say YES.'

5

The Meaning of the Word Amen

Jews, Christians, and Muslims have been using the word Amen for thousands of years. Before we look deeper into what the word Amen means, I will first explain, concisely, the nature of God.

There is one God and this one God is indivisible. As God is indivisible, God can never be antithetical. All is one. Your intellect defines everything that enters your awareness in terms of antitheses. Your intellect is unable to describe something as it is truly perceived. That is why your intellect is incapable of understanding God. Still, you can understand God, not with your intellect but with your heart.

We can attribute three aspects to God, which is solely for your intellect that is incapable of understanding that God is indivisible.

The first aspect is male. It is God the Father. It is the source from which everything originates. God the Father is the Creator of all things. Everything that exists comes forth from God the Father and everything returns to him. In itself, God the Father is void. It is the infinite, everlasting, unchangeable truth.

The second aspect is female. It is God the Mother and also called the Spirit or Holy Ghost. God the Mother is the force that comes forth from God the Father. She is the power that makes the Creation possible, the life energy that nurtures all that is created. She can be understood as knowledge and wisdom (Gnosis). She can be felt as love and perceived as light in visions. From now on, I will call this aspect of God 'the Love Light of God the Mother'.

The third aspect is God the Son. God the Son is the entire Creation but it is also every part of the Creation, including every human being. God the Son comes forth from God the Father and consists of the Love Light. In the Bible, the Gospel of John begins with the words:

> *In the beginning was the Word, and the Word was with God, and the Word was God. He was with God in the beginning. Through him all things were made; without him nothing was made that has been made. In him was life, and that life was the light of all mankind. The light shines in the darkness, and the darkness has not overcome it.*
> (Gospel of John 1:1-5)

This means that the Love Light of God the Mother is in the Creator and that the Love Light of God the Mother is the light of mankind.

So what is this particular word that was with God in the beginning? This word (the Logos) symbolises the beginning of every act of creation. It is an act of God the Father, the Creator, that leads to Creation as such. The Bible uses the term 'Word' but it could also have been described as 'Sound'. What matters is that it is the Creator's first act that culminates in Creation. It is God saying, 'Yes.'

The creating word 'Yes' spoken by God the Father is symbolised by the guttural sound AA-OO-MM. This sound starts by making the sound AA followed by slowly closing your mouth, and when you let the sound roll forward through your mouth and your lips are nearly closed, the AA sounds become OO. When your lips close, all that is left of the sound is MM. As the sound in your mouth rolls forward, the word is formed by all the different sounds. That is why the word AA-OO-MM symbolises all the sounds made by the Creator, or all the Yes words said by God that culminate in Creation and, as such, also becomes the symbol of Creation itself.

In Hebrew, the word AA-OO-MM is written as a word that

literally says OO-MM, but which is pronounced in Judaism and Christianity as AMEN. In Islam, the word is pronounced as AMIN, and in Hinduism and Buddhism as OM. People often think that Amen originally is a Hebrew word but that is not the case. Abraham was a Brahmin. He came from India and his name also refers to Brahma: A-Brahm and he brought the symbol to the Middle East.

The word Amen also comes with a symbol. For that, we look at the three aspects of God and their symbols.

The first aspect is God the Father, the Creator. The symbol for God the Father is a circle. A circle has a centre and its circumference is infinite. The number that is linked to this is 1.

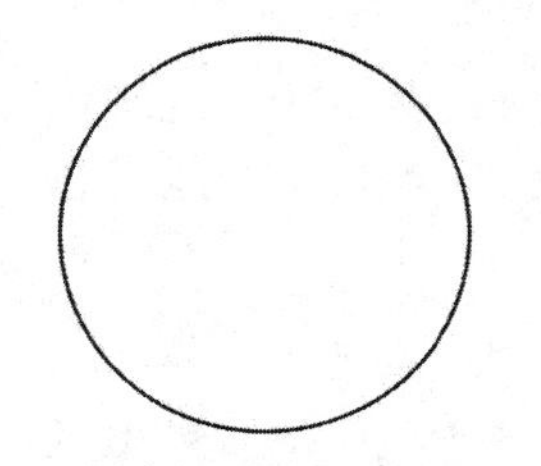

Figure 1. God the Father

The second aspect is the Love Light of God the Mother. The symbol for the Love Light of God the Mother is an ellipse. An ellipse can be constructed by having two focal points, two centres. The number that is linked to this is 2. An ellipse is also the shape and symbol for the womb, the female organ in which Creation will originate. The ellipse is fully enclosed by the circle.

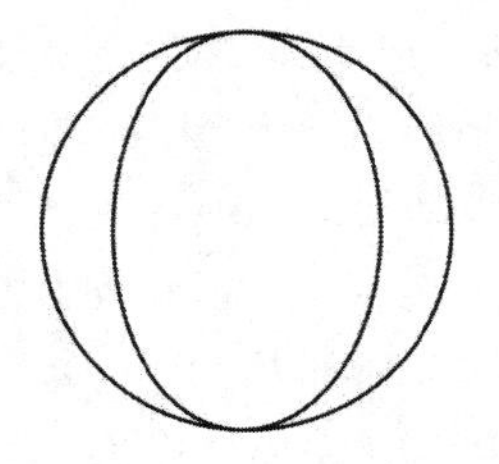

Figure 2. God the Mother

The third aspect is God the Son, or Creation. Creation originates from the Creator and is made of the Love Light of God the Mother. The symbol for Creation is a foetus, a baby, tucked inside the ellipse as a foetus in the womb.

Figure 3. God the Son

The heart of the foetus coincides exactly with the centre of the circle. The heart of man is the heart of God.

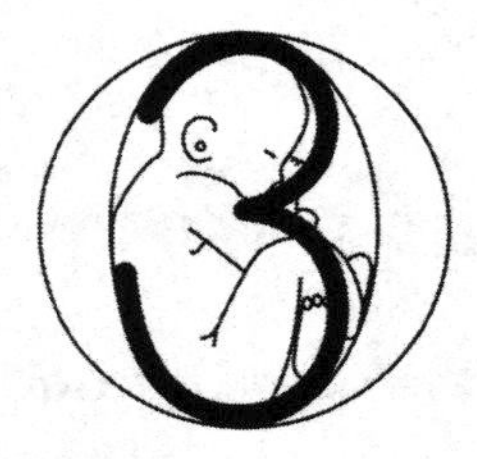

Figure 4. The symbol for Creation is 3.

In the Bible, the word Yes spoken by God is symbolised as the Word that was in the beginning. This word, in turn, can be symbolised by the word AA-OO-MM that includes all sounds. And ultimately, the word AA-OO-MM can be symbolised by the symbol 3. This word is pronounced as Amen.

The symbol is much wider known in Hinduism and Buddhism. The heart of the foetus is connected with the edge of the circle by some sort of umbilical cord, which is a symbolic depiction of the human heart being connected with the infiniteness of the all-encompassing Creator. Opposite the human head are a crescent moon and a star, symbolising wisdom and knowledge.

Figure 5. Om

So to recap, the word Amen symbolises the first Word spoken by God, Yes. It is the act of God that culminates in Creation and which confirms Creation. It also symbolises Creation itself, and the written symbol is our number 3 as well as the Hindu sign Om.

El Jazim means: God-Yes-Be. El represents God the Father, Ja represents God the Mother and Zim represents God the Son. The name El Jazim contains all aspects of God and it is God's Yes to you.

Amen also contains all aspects of God. It includes God the Father (1), God the Mother (2) and God the Son (3). Amen therefore also contains all aspects of God and it is your yes to God.

The name El Jazim is the 33rd name of God. The reason for that is that the number 33 is the highest number in numerology. It consists of 3-3, or Amen-Amen. It is the symbol for the greatest and the highest. It is also the symbol for Christ.

Jews can go into the Holy of Holies to speak the name of God, and if they do, their sins are forgiven.

Christians are hallowed if they speak the name of God.

Muslims submit themselves to God. If you submit yourself to God, you are a Muslim. If you speak the name of God and you confirm it by speaking Amen to God, with all of your mind, with all of your heart and with all of your soul, then you are a

Muslim. Then you open your heart for the Yes word of God and you will enter paradise.

EL JAZIM, EL JAZIM, EL JAZIM
AMEN

6

The Name of Christ and the Coming of the Messiah

If Creation is the result of God saying Yes, then Creation is entirely within God the Father and consists of the Love Light of God the Mother. The entire Creation and every part of it is created in the image of God. Creation, and every part of it, is inspired by the Love Light of God and has, in itself, the power to create.

Every person has a soul. Every soul is created by God. As every person has a soul, so all animals, plants, and even atoms have souls. Planets and stars have souls. The name of Earth's soul is Gaiael, or Gaia. The name of the soul of our solar system is Ishmael. The universe has a soul too. The name of the soul of the universe is Christiel, or Christ.

Sometimes, Christ sends a prophet to Earth. A prophet is a person with extraordinary talents and who has been part of Christ's power. Moses, Jesus, and Mohammed were all prophets, but there were more.

And very rarely, Christ himself comes to Earth. This person has all of Christ's power vested in him.

The Jews expect that Christ will come to Earth and they call him the Messiah.

Christians expect that Jesus will return to Earth. Christians sometimes confuse Jesus with Christ as they think that they are one and the same, as Jesus is also called Jesus Christ. But his soul is not the soul of the universe and so his name is not Christ. Jesus was named Christ because the name was given to him as a title. It is an honorary title for him to carry because, thanks to him, the Christ-awareness came into full bloom and the Christ-energy flooded through him into the world. Jesus lived entirely in Christ-awareness and he had overcome all his personal inclinations. He was a Christ-person.

Muslims also await the second coming of Christ and call him the Messiah. Some schools of theology or movements believe that the returned Jesus will assist the also expected Mahdi, the twelfth Caliph who will lead all Muslims. Other schools of theology believe that the Messiah and the Mahdi are one and the same person.

I can assure you that the Messiah will come. He is also the Mahdi who is expected by the Muslims. His coming will be announced by the person who will reveal the last name of God by the end of times.

As you have read in this book, I have announced the last name of God and hereby I also announce the coming of the Messiah, just as it is foretold. The end time has begun and the Messiah is coming. He is already here but he has yet to reveal himself. He is still a small child today but he will reveal himself when he is old enough. As my messages will touch your heart and restore the foundations of Judaism, Christianity, and Islam, the Messiah will not only touch your heart but He will restore the foundations of all religions on Earth. On this foundation, he will build a house, a house of Love Light where you will find a room.

The Messiah will be the leader of all Muslims. That doesn't mean he will be an earthly leader. He will be a spiritual leader of all people who surrender themselves to God, because those people are the real Muslims whether they are Jewish, Christian, Muslim, Buddhist, Hindu or otherwise religious.

I tell you: the Messiah has come but he has yet to reveal himself. But when he reveals himself, he will be easily recognised. You only have to look into his eyes. His eyes will be overflowing with love, the Love of God.

To prepare for his arrival, I bring you a message from the Messiah. These are the Messiah's own words:

Dearly beloved,
Your heart and my heart,
is one heart,
it's the heart of all,
it's the heart of God.

7

The seven Spirits and the Elders

1 The seven Spirits

There is one God and this one God is indivisible.

As God is indivisible, God can never be antithetical. All is one. Your intellect defines everything that enters the awareness in terms of antitheses. Your intellect is unable to describe something as it is truly perceived. That is why your intellect is incapable of understanding God. Still, you can understand God, not with your intellect but with your heart.

We can attribute three aspects to God: God the Father, God the Mother, and God the Son, which is solely for your intellect that is incapable of understanding that God is indivisible.

God the Father is the Creator. He is the source from which everything comes forth.

God the Mother comes forth from God the Father and is the Love Light.

God the Son is Creation and every part of it, and consists entirely of the Love Light.

The name of God is El Jazim. This means 'God-yes-be'. This name refers to the creative power of God. It is the word Yes spoken by God that culminates in Creation. El Jazim is the first and last of God's names. Amen confirms all God's features and is your 'yes' to God.

Creation is the result of God saying Yes. It is important to know that Creation is not something that happened at some point in the past, and that it has developed independently ever since. You are living in the here and now, and Creation happens at every indivisible moment in the here and now.

We can attribute two aspects to Creation: creation and destruction, which is solely for your intellect that is incapable of understanding that God is indivisible, and that the here and now is timeless.

Creation happens at every moment in the here and now, through the creative act of God, symbolised by him saying Yes, and at every moment in the here and now, Creation is also destroyed. Only the here and now really exists. The here and now is also infinitely small and changes continuously. In terms of antitheses, it is the untruth that is the antithesis of the truth. It is the form that is the antithesis of formlessness.

Creation of every moment in the here and now occurs by God the Father saying Yes. And from God the Father stems the Love Light of God the Mother. Creation consists of the Love Light of God the Mother and is therefore called God the Son.

As light is made of seven colours and sound consists of seven root sounds, the Love Light of God the Mother is made of seven root frequencies. These are the seven Spirits of God that John saw in the Book of Revelation (3.1, 4.5 and 5.6). But there is only one Elohim: El Jazim, because there is only one God. The entire Creation is made of the seven Spirits of God, because the entire Creation is made of the Love Light of God the Mother.

Symbolically, the seven Spirits of God can be represented as seven beams of light radiating from one focal point. This focal point is El. El is God the Father. The beams form the Love Light of God the Mother.

2 The Elders

Souls are created in waves. Long before Earth was created and long before the souls of Earth People were created, a wave of souls was created. These souls dispersed throughout the universe and 24 of them came to the still non-existing Earth. They are the 24 'Elders' described by John in the Book of Revelation. This is how John describes it in the Book of Revelation:

> [2]*At once I was in the Spirit, and there before me was a throne in heaven with someone sitting on it.* [3]*And the one who sat there had the appearance of jasper and ruby. A rainbow that shone like an emerald encircled the throne.* [4]*Surrounding the throne were twenty-four other thrones, and seated on them were twenty-four elders. They were dressed in white and had crowns of gold on their heads.*
> (Book of Revelation 4:2-4)

These 24 Elders helped to prepare Earth to receive life and they brought life to Earth. When plants and animals already inhabited Earth but mankind did not yet exist, they led the Devas, or angels, who guided the different lifeforms. Later on, when people had come into existence as well, they assumed roles such as priests, kings, and prophets to help mankind. They sometimes presented themselves to humans as archangels.

All Elders, meaning all archangels, were created simultaneously and are equal in rank. They are neither male nor female but can adopt the shape of a man or woman as it suits them. The Elders are souls who don't have to be worshipped although you can pray to them. Still, it is better to pray directly to God. When your prayers are sincere, the powers that are needed for your prayers to be answered will come of their own accord.

Some of the Elders may choose to live a life as a human, to help carrying out a particular task or gain experiences as a person so they are better able to understand and help other humans. Rulers on Earth, in turn, are eager to kill these archangel-humans, or to declare them insane or demonise them. They are wrong to do so. They are Love Light beings who spread their unconditional love and only wish to help you.

Perhaps you now think that archangels are some sort of higher and better beings. They are not. Archangels have a soul, as you have a soul. In the core of your being, you are an angel too because you are not the equivalent of your soul but a sliver of God's awareness, just like the archangels. They are not higher or better beings but they are much, much older in Earth years because they were created in an earlier soul wave. That's why they have gained more experiences. You may see them as older brothers and sisters. After all, we all have the same Father.

8

The Purpose of Life and the First Commandment

The purpose of life is to grow in love. That is why the first commandment says: Love God above all else and your neighbour as yourself. You feel love when your heart overflows. When your heart overflows with love, you feel the Love Light of God. Love is your connection with God.

God created you by saying Yes. God says Yes to you for all eternity and unconditionally. You are God's love.

When you love, you feel happy. When you love, you say 'yes'. Saying 'no' will make you unhappy. When you say 'no', you close yourself off and love stops. But no matter how hard you say 'no' and no matter how unhappy you are, the Love Light of God the Mother is poured out on you. Yes, on you too. The Love Light of God is the water of life. It is the well that you drink from freely. Every person has a free will. You can say 'yes' and love, or you can say 'no' and close yourself off. But no matter if you say 'yes' or 'no', God's love is with you always.

Besides love, there is another path that leads to God. This path is called submission. Those who submit completely to God are reborn in Christ. This is what 'dying to the world' means. It is the death of the ego. It is the death that we must go through to find life.

Jews have to pass through the Dead Sea, which also symbolises the death of the ego. Submersion in the water of death precedes life.

Christians first need to die before they can live. It is what Jesus taught his followers. Those who die to their egos are reborn in Christ and come to life.

Muslims must also submit themselves to God. Islam means

'submission' and those who submit to God are Muslims.

So Judaism, Christianity, and Islam are not that different when it comes to this fundamental, inherent element. The differences mostly concern external matters. Jews, Christians, and Muslims believe in the same God. His name is El Jazim. Jews, Christians, and Muslims confirm their prayers by saying Amen. Jews, Christians, and Muslims live by the same first commandment, which is to love God above all else and your neighbour as yourself. Jews have to pass through the Dead Sea, Christians must die to their ego so they will live, and Muslims must submit themselves to God. These are all the same things. It means letting go of your ego. It is the death of your ego and putting God above all else, and submitting everything to Him. It is saying 'yes' to God and the transition from the ego-centred awareness to a heart-centred awareness.

Mohammed said that all people will become Muslims when the Messiah comes. That doesn't mean that all people on Earth will convert to Islam. Whoever submits to God is considered a Muslim, also when they are Jewish or Christian. Mohammed also said that he is the last prophet. And this is true. After Mohammed, no other prophet has appeared before the Jews, Christians, or Muslims. However, there have been messengers. I am one of them but I am not a prophet, and after me, the Messiah will come. So Mohammed spoke truthfully.

There is no need to fear the coming of the Messiah. The Messiah will wield great power but his power is not of this world. He will not rule the world like a monarch but his love will encompass all of the Earth and all of mankind like a glove fits around a hand. He will also not judge you. Neither God nor the Messiah will judge. You will only judge yourself. You have the choice of 'yes' or 'no', at every moment of every day. And you have the choice to love, or not, at every moment of every day. That is the judgement.

Moreover, I bear a message from God to you. This message

is not directed at your intellect but rather at your heart. Your intellect will not be able to understand the message but your heart will.

The message starts with the words: 'Beloved Son'. God the Son is Creation and every part of it. Whoever you are, wherever you are, whatever you do, you are the Son of God. You are the Son of God, regardless of your gender, your religion, your nature or orientation, the colour of your skin, your age, or your appearance. It doesn't matter what you do, or did in the past, whether you are healthy or sick. It doesn't matter if you are scared, angry, or sad, and it even doesn't matter if you believe in God or not. This message is for you. These are God's own words:

Beloved Son,
I am the eternal, unchanging, absolute Existence.
I am your life and you are my consciousness.
That is why I am your Father and you are my Son.
Where consciousness and life merge,
there is nothing but pure happiness.
This happiness is my grace that I pour out upon you unfalteringly.
El Jazim

9

The Foundations of Judaism, Christianity, and Islam

In the previous chapters, I restored the common foundations of Judaism, Christianity, and Islam. This foundations can be summarised as follows:

1. There is one God and this one God is indivisible. There are three aspects of God: God the Father, God the Mother, and God the Son. God the Father is the Creator. He is the source from which everything comes forth. God the Mother comes forth from God the Father and is the Love Light. This Love Light is made of seven root frequencies. God the Son is Creation and every part of it, and consists entirely of the Love Light.
2. The first and last name of God is El Jazim. This means 'God-yes-be'. This name symbolises God speaking the word Yes, which culminates in Creation.
3. Amen is the word by which the trinity of God the Father, God the Mother, and God the Son is confirmed. It is you saying 'yes' to God.
4. Christ is the name of the soul of the universe. He sent the prophets. All who submit themselves to God and say 'yes' to God from the heart will be reborn in Christ.
5. The awaited Messiah is the coming of Christ on Earth. The Messiah has come but has yet to reveal himself. He will restore the foundations of all religions on Earth and encompass Earth with the Love Light.
6. There are 24 Elders who brought life to Earth and who help mankind in their growth process. They are the archangels.

7. The purpose of life is to 'grow in love'. The first commandment says: 'Love God above all else and your neighbour as yourself.'

I now have restored the foundations of Judaism, Christianity, and Islam, and I have announced the coming of the Messiah. I declare to you that I have restored and explained the foundations of Judaism, Christianity, and Islam to the best of my knowledge. However, should my words ever seem to contradict the words spoken by the Messiah, then believe the Messiah because my power and talents are only limited. He will come with great power and his talents are infinite because he is the Christ.

I call on everyone to live by these foundations, Jews, Christians, and Muslims alike, and to build your synagogue, church, or mosque on this foundations. Prepare yourself for the coming of the Messiah because I tell you now: he is already among us.

10

The Path to a Heart-Centred Awareness

The human race is now facing the challenge to transfer from an ego-centred awareness to a heart-centred awareness. It is a process, a path to be taken, which goes through different stages. I call this path 'The Path to a Heart-centred Awareness', or simply 'the Path'.

Over the centuries, there have always been small groups of Jews, Christians, and Muslims who wish to grow spiritually. Their Path to a heart-centred awareness is based on the holy scriptures, and experiences and teachings of more advanced teachers. This Path is only known to the members of these private groups and often only revealed to those who were initiated. This is why such teachings are called 'esoteric', which means 'hidden'. Members of such groups were often prosecuted and killed. As these groups were relatively small and private, the knowledge that was taught varied greatly as well, and so there is not one esoteric teaching. Nevertheless, the different esoteric systems all share the same foundation.

The Path to a heart-centred awareness follows seven stages, which will be described later on. For now, it is important to understand the development that is hidden behind the seven stages of the Path. It is the development from an ego-centred awareness to a heart-centred awareness. It is a common denominator incorporated in all of the seven stages. I will first describe this common denominator. After that, I will explain the concept of the soul and then the seven development stages.

The essence of God, of life, of love, of the Christ awareness is 'Existence-Consciousness-Bliss'. Any person who lives from the heart-centred awareness finds himself in this state of Existence-Consciousness-Bliss. In Sanskrit, this is called 'Sat-

Chit-Ananda', a state that comes forth of oneness. Existence-Consciousness-Bliss is your natural state and you don't need to do anything to be in this state. It is your true nature and it is actually very odd that you are not constantly in this state of Existence-Consciousness-Bliss. The fact that you are not is caused by your ego-centred awareness. Your ego developed some very powerful instruments to avoid being in this state of oneness and remain in a state of separation. Consequently, you are living in an illusion that blocks the state of Existence-Consciousness-Bliss.

For the individual states of Existence, Consciousness, and Bliss, the ego created instruments that block you from entering this state. They will be hereunder and I will explain how to destroy those instruments, which you can employ within your own life straight away. Chapter 13 Practical Instructions to Follow the Path will also provide you with some more practical instructions that may help along the Path.

1 Existence

Existence is a state of spontaneous and creative development. It is the here and now of Creation as it develops and unfolds in a completely natural and unobstructed manner. The instrument that the ego uses to prevent you from entering this state is by exerting power. Power is the antithesis of love when we believe that love cannot exist wherever power is exerted, and love rules where no power is exerted. Power is the capability to influence your environment via your will. Your will is rooted in your abdomen, just below your diaphragm, also called the solar plexus. This is where the centre of your ego resides and from where you exert power over your environment through your will. Your will is like a beam of energy coming from your solar plexus, which literally bounces against Creation to change and adjust it. In doing so, you frustrate the spontaneous, creative development of Creation and of the Love Light of God.

The exertion of power creates tension between what you want and the natural process of Creation. This tension, in turn, puts you in a constant state of stress while you desperately try to achieve something that goes against Creation and God's Will. Something may lead to temporary success but when Creation continues on its natural course, everything you have achieved will collapse like a house of cards.

Your heart totally goes against your will because it doesn't send an energy flow as an instrument of power to control Creation. Your heart receives what it encounters, embraces it, and loves it. Your heart doesn't want to change what is. Your heart trusts that whatever Creation brings you will be perfect and good. Your heart surrounds itself with everything that rises up from your awareness from love so it can all grow, bloom, and come to fruition naturally.

All you should do is stop exerting power and stop fighting against what Creation brings you. You can love and trust, and let be what is. It will release you from the stressed state of desiring and bring you into the relaxed state of loving. The motto that goes with it is: 'go with the flow'.

2 Consciousness

You think that you live from your consciousness, but you often don't. Living from your consciousness is being fully present and aware in the here and now. It means perceiving without having thoughts, emotions, and judgement. You just are but you are also aware that you are.

The instruments that the ego uses to prevent you from entering this state of Consciousness are thoughts, emotions, and judgements. Thoughts never cease to go through your head. They are mostly about the past or the future, about the things you have done, or have to do. However, most thoughts rarely are very constructive. Thoughts succeed each other so rapidly that it seems that there is no space between the separate thoughts.

Still, between two thoughts, there is a small moment of space. You can start looking for that space, and when you recognise it, you can hold on to that space. You can learn to enlarge this space to create holes between your thoughts in which you are aware, and truly in the here and now.

You also constantly have negative emotions, and you feel as if you can drown in them. The main negative emotions are fear, anger, depression, and sadness, although, ultimately, all negative emotions are rooted in fear. The core of fear is the ingrained fear of dying. Your ego doesn't want to die. Your ego also doesn't want to change as any change is the death of something that is. But life is nothing but change. Life and death go hand in hand. They are two sides of the same coin. In reality, only the coin exists. It is the here and now. And the here and now changes constantly whereas the ego considers this as death. The ego fears death, and you get angry because you think that this may drown out the fear so you don't have to face it. You start to focus your urge to destroy what you believe is causing your misery, and you wallow in the energy that is released because of this. In some cases, your urge to destroy gets aimed at yourself and you become depressed or, in very serious cases, even suicidal, which is not a solution because something inside you is unchangeable. It is the core of your existence. It is a tiny bit of God. It is your consciousness in which Creation rises and goes down again, and it is something you can't escape from.

The solution is to focus your attention on your abdomen. That is where the energies that fuel your emotions are located, and where you can face your emotions and embrace them. You can experience them, feel them, and release them. The best way of doing this is by looking at them from a distance. By observing them without losing yourself in them, which may sound easy but really is not. You need to overcome yourself to achieve this. Sometimes, you manage to do it on your own while in other cases you need the help of a friend or a healthcare specialist like a professional therapist. There is absolutely no shame in facing your emotions and seeing a therapist. On the contrary, it is a brave and wise choice to make, and it can be a major step in your development.

Another powerful instrument used by the ego is judgement. When you judge, you set yourself apart from what you convict and it also creates strong emotions. You divide Creation between good and bad although, ultimately, you are only judging yourself. The solution for this is to love without judgement. 'Judge not lest ye be judged yourself.' This doesn't refer to you being judged by someone else. Every moment you judge something or someone, you judge yourself.

3 Bliss

Bliss is the natural state you find yourself in when you are completely satisfied and happy with yourself and your circumstances. You are happy when you say 'yes' to Creation wholeheartedly.

The instrument that the ego uses to prevent you from entering this state of Bliss is by seeking happiness and satisfaction in outer appearances and situations. You feel a desire to own something and will do everything to get it. You experience a moment of happiness as soon as you get it, but this feeling is short-lived and then you start wanting something new. You want to go on holiday, another job, a bigger house, more money, another partner and you keep on searching and striving for satisfaction. But in the outer world and circumstances, you will never find anything that will give you everlasting happiness. Seeking satisfaction and happiness in outer circumstances is basically saying 'no' to your inner self, and to the here and now. The search is a bottomless pit of greediness and attachment, and you will feel anger or jealousy as soon as the moment of happiness turns into unhappiness.

The only solution is making sure that the ego gives up this

search, and then start looking at your inner self. The only source of everlasting satisfaction will be found within yourself. You will be happy when you wholeheartedly say 'yes' to yourself and the circumstances you are in.

Existence-Consciousness-Bliss is your natural state. You only have to let go of everything that isn't real or which exists anyway. Love, trust, and submission are the path to Existence-Consciousness-Bliss. This is the essence of your true self. This is the Christ-awareness. It is the inheritance that is waiting for you because you are a child of God.

4 The Soul

You have a soul. Your soul was created by God the Father. After your soul was created, it still remained one with God. The soul is made of the Love Light and, like God the Father, it is capable of creating. As it has a need to create, your soul was drawn to a place where it can create and experience its individuality. For the Earth souls, this place is Earth. For the lightbringers, it first was another place.

Your soul has a goal, which is gaining experiences and thus grow in love and awareness. Most people's souls, the Earth souls, now find themselves in a stage where they learn what it is like to individualise and separate from their unity with God. They live in an ego-centred awareness. In reality, nobody can separate themselves from this unity as every soul is entirely one with God, consisting of the Love Light of God, and they can never leave God. So with your thoughts, you create an illusion of separation that doesn't exist and can never exist in real life.

The concept that I explained above may have you thinking that the process of creation happens in time. But this is actually not the case, as the entire creative process of the entire Creation and every part of it happens in the here and now. In Genesis, the creation of the soul is described as follows:

And God said, 'Let us make man in our image, after our likeness. And let them have dominion over the fish of the sea and over the birds of the heavens and over the livestock and over all the earth and over every creeping thing that creeps on the earth.' So God created man in his own image, in the image of God he created him; male and female he created them.
(Genesis 1:26-27)

and

These are the generations of the heavens and the earth when they were created, in the day that the LORD God made the earth and the heavens. When no bush of the field was yet in the land and no small plant of the field had yet sprung up—for the LORD God had not caused it to rain on the land, and there was no man to work the ground, and a mist was going up from the land and was watering the whole face of the ground. Then the LORD God formed the man of dust from the ground and breathed into his nostrils the breath of life, and the man became a living creature.
(Genesis 2:4-7)

After your soul was created, it still remained one with God. It was light within light but then, in some places, the light got a little more dense and duality and antitheses appeared. Adam and Eve, the souls who first lived in the Garden of Eden, meaning in unity with God, slowly learn about antithesis, about good and evil.

And Jahwe God commanded them as follows: You may surely eat of every tree of the garden, but of the tree of the knowledge of good and evil you shall not eat, for in the day that you eat of it you shall surely die.
(Genesis 2:16-17)

and:

And the woman said to the serpent, 'We may eat of the fruit of the trees in the garden, but God said, "You shall not eat of the fruit of the tree that is in the midst of the garden, neither shall you touch it, lest you die."' But the serpent said to the woman, 'You will not surely die. For God knows that when you eat of it your eyes will be opened, and you will be like God, knowing good and evil.'
(Genesis 3:2-4)

But Adam and Eve cannot restrain themselves. They eat of the apple and learn about good and evil. And after they learn about good and evil, they are expelled from the Garden of Eden. This means that they, by having knowledge of antitheses, were taken away from their blissful state. The same happens to Lucifer, the Morningstar who falls from heaven.

How you are fallen from heaven, O Day Star, son of Dawn! How you are cut down to the ground, you who laid the nations low! You said in your heart, 'I will ascend to heaven; above the stars of God, I will set my throne on high; I will sit on the mount of assembly in the far reaches of the north; I will ascend above the heights of the clouds; I will make myself like the Highest.' But you are brought down to Sheol, to the far reaches of the pit.
(Isaiah 14:12-14)

Also, Ezekiel spoke about this when he addresses the King of Tyre:

So says God: You were the signet of perfection, full of wisdom and perfect in beauty. You were in Eden, the garden of God; every precious stone was your covering, sardius, topaz, and diamond, beryl, onyx, and jasper, sapphire, emerald, and carbuncle; and crafted in gold were your settings and your engravings. On

> *the day that you were created they were prepared. You were an anointed guardian cherub. I placed you; you were on the holy mountain of God; in the midst of the stones of fire you walked. You were blameless in your ways from the day you were created, till unrighteousness was found in you.*
> (Ezekiel 28:12-15)

Isaiah and Ezekiel both describe the fall from paradise. The creation of the soul which is first one with God, with the light, but then sets himself apart and individualises. The fallen angel is your soul, and it is mine. You have a soul that was created and then separated itself from the oneness. Please understand that this doesn't say that you are a devil, or evil, or a sinner. It only means to say that you follow your desire to explore, discover, and create. It is a growth path as it was meant by your Creator, God the Father.

Adam and Eve symbolise all of mankind. Your soul was expelled from paradise but it can also return to it. It is a cycle. Jacob perceived this cycle when he saw angels come down a ladder from heaven and rise up again to heaven (Genesis 28:10-12).

> *Jacob left Beersheba and went towards Haran. And he came to a certain place and stayed there that night, because the sun had set. Taking one of the stones of the place, he put it under his head and lay down in that place to sleep. And he dreamed, and behold, there was a ladder set up on the earth, and the top of it reached to heaven. And behold, the angels of God were ascending and descending on it!*

The angels come down the ladder and go up again to return to heaven. You are not your body, or your ego. You are your soul. Your soul, meaning you, only expresses itself in your life, your body, your ego. You are an angel too, who descended the ladder and who may return to heaven by ascending the ladder again. For as long as you wish to experience your individuality and want to be separated from God, you will remain in the outward movement. You go down the ladder and you find yourself in the ego-centred phase. Some angels only come down a small way and then choose to return. Others descend very deep before they return. The deeper the descent, the harder it will be to return. Yet, all angels return to heaven. No matter how deep you find yourself, you will always be an angel from heaven.

> *The Lord fulfil his purpose for me; your steadfast love, O Lord, endures forever. Do not forsake the work of your hands.*
> (Psalm 138:8, but in the Dutch version it says: *'... and Who does not forsake the work that His divine hand began.'*)

The transition from the ego-centred awareness to a heart-centred awareness is the return of the angels up Jacob's ladder, back to heaven. Lucifer, the Morningstar, who will shine his light again in all its glory. Adam and Eve, who will give up their knowledge of good and evil and return to paradise. This is not some other person's path. It is your path. It is your right to claim your inheritance as a Son of God. It is your right to return to paradise. To a new heaven and a new Earth. The Bible tells us of another parable that not only describes the fall from paradise but also the return to it. It is the parable of the prodigal son.

> *He said: 'There was a man who had two sons. The younger one said to his father, "Father, give me my share of the estate." So he divided his property between them. Not long after that, the younger son collected all he had, set off for a distant country, and there he squandered his wealth by living recklessly. After he had spent everything, the entire country was struck by a severe famine and he began to be in need. So he went and hired himself out to a citizen of that country, who sent him to his fields to herd the pigs.*

And although he longed to fill his stomach with the peels that the pigs were eating, no one gave him anything. When he came to his senses, he said, "How many of my father's hired servants have food to spare while I am here, starving to death! I will set out and go back to my father and say to him: Father, I have sinned against heaven and against you; I am no longer worthy to be called your son but hire me as one of your servants." So he went away, back to his father. While he was still a long way off, his father saw him and was filled with compassion for him; he ran to his son, threw his arms around him and kissed him. The son said to him, "Father, I have sinned against heaven and against you. I am no longer worthy to be called your son." But the father said to his servants, "Hurry! Bring the best robe and put it on him. Put a ring on his finger and sandals on his feet. Bring the fattened calf and kill it. Let's have a feast and celebrate, because this son of mine was dead and is alive again; he was lost and is found." So they began to celebrate. Meanwhile, the older son was in the field. But when he came near the house, he heard music and dancing. He called one of the servants and asked him what was going on. The servant answered, "Your brother has come home and your father has killed the fattened calf because he has him back safe and sound." The older brother became angry and refused to go in. When his father came out and pleaded with him, he gave his father the following answer: "All these years I've been slaving for you and never disobeyed your orders. Yet you never gave me even a young goat so I could celebrate with my friends. But when this son of yours who has squandered your property with lewd women comes home, you kill the fattened calf for him." And then the father answered, "My son, you are always with me, and everything I have is yours. But we had to celebrate and be merry because this brother of yours was dead and is alive again; he was lost and is found."'

(Luke 15:11-32)

Moses, Jesus, Mohammed, and many others have preceded you

in the return to your origin, which is named the Kingdom of God. It is a path that you can take as well, or rather must take, whether you want to or not. Everything must return to the source from whence it came. All the angels that Jacob saw ascended the ladder, up to heaven. Every person has an ingrained longing, inside his heart, to be one with God. So it is not about if you will return but when, because you being one with God is where you belong. Deep inside your heart, you know this. That is why your heart calls out: 'Come, beloved, come.'

11

The Seven Stages of the Path

The Path to a heart-centred awareness follows the next seven stages:

Stage 1 Coming to faith
Stage 2 Coming to repentance
Stage 3 Submission to God and rebirth in Christ
Stage 4 Becoming one with God the Mother
Stage 5 Becoming one with God the Father
Stage 6 Becoming one with God the Son
Stage 7 Christ-awareness

These stages are not definite and should be considered somewhat loosely. You may require fewer or more stages. Sometimes, you skip a stage and take a step back later on. The stages may be described otherwise and the development can also be described differently. This is why I will not discuss the different stages extensively. They should be seen as a foundation to give shape to further thoughts and insights, and to create bridges to different ideas about spiritual development.

The reason as to why I distinguish these seven stages has everything to do with the fact that this coincides best with the development stages described in the Bible. Moreover, they tie in well with the development stages used in transpersonal psychology. It allows for making the connection between Christianity and transpersonal psychology.

One of the aspects of all seven development stages is personal growth. The growth pattern through every stage of the Path is the same as that of the psychological development stages. I will also explain this growth pattern. The purpose of explaining the growth pattern is to link the Path to a heart-centred awareness and the scientific aspect of development psychology so that the Path can be researched and, thus, find a way to connect religion, spiritual development, development psychology, and transpersonal psychology.

This chapter describes the seven stages of the Path to a heart-centred awareness. The next chapter focuses on the growth patterns within each stage.

Stage 1 Coming to Faith

Your soul is made of the Love Light of God the Mother, and is entirely one with God. When the influence of the soul grows to such an extent that this influence penetrates the illusions and thoughts of your ego and enters your awareness, then a person comes to faith. This insight can come as a bolt of lightning. A sudden moment in which you realise that God exists. You don't think that God exists, you know that he does. There is no doubt in your mind. Suddenly you know: 'God is real'. You don't necessarily have to come to faith in God. You can also come to faith in some other power, in love, in an energy field, or in something else. But one thing is sure, the moment you come to faith, you will never doubt again. And as long as you haven't come to faith, there will always be doubt. It is also possible that you have always believed in God but never experienced this sudden moment of insight. What counts is that the influence of your soul is so strong that faith is a given fact for you.

Stage 2 Coming to Repentance

Coming to repentance is a conscious decision to turn your life to God. The moment of coming to faith and coming to repentance may happen simultaneously, but it doesn't have to. You can come to faith without wanting to come to repentance. Repentance is a decision taken freely and consciously, based on personal motives such as the wish to build up credit with God.

When you come to repentance, you basically put your faith in God at the top of your list of priorities, but it still remains a list of priorities of the ego.

Stage 3 Submission to God and Rebirth in Christ

Rebirth in Christ happens at the moment that you realise deep inside your heart that you, personally, can do absolutely nothing to achieve something but that everything is in the hands of God. This is when you fully submit yourself to God. This insight will hit you at an unexpected moment and there is no doubt in your mind that your ego is truly powerless, and that all your attempts to reach eternal happiness have failed and will keep failing in the future. At this moment of submitting yourself to God, you accept the death of your ego and you are reborn in Christ. This rebirth in Christ is a fully conscious awareness. You know that you are reborn because you feel this rebirth happening.

As long as you still believe that you can achieve anything to increase your happiness with your ego, you haven't yet been reborn in Christ.

In the Bible, the moment of rebirth in Christ is the moment when the angels who descend Jacob's ladder turn around and go back up the ladder again. It is also the moment when the prodigal son 'comes to his senses' and realises that he should return to his father. It is the moment that you are no longer descended from Adam, the first man, but descended from Jesus, the second man. It is the birth of the Christ-awareness.

After you have come to repentance, you still identify yourself with the ego. This continues until the moment that the ego submits and you are then reborn in Christ. After being reborn in Christ, the identification with the ego slowly diminishes. That doesn't mean that your ego disappears. Your ego will still exist, but from the moment that you are reborn in Christ, it is the identification with your ego that will cease. This is the moment that a new person, a new soul, or the Christ-awareness is born.

The Christ-awareness was always there under the surface, but from now on, the identification with the Christ-awareness grows. It is something that is barely perceivable at first. The Christ-awareness is like a baby but it will grow slowly. When all the seven stages are completed, the identification with the ego ceases to exist and you live fully in the Christ-awareness. You have completely released the identification with your ego.

Submitting yourself to God is the most difficult moment in your life and in the existence of your soul because you, as your ego, accept your own death. You relinquish that which you always believed yourself to be, and put yourself and your life in God's hands. It is a real turning point whereby the separation from God turns into a convergence with God. But no matter how difficult it is, it will happen when you are ready. It is not a rational choice. It is a decision taken naturally when the moment of insight hits you.

Stage 4 Becoming One with God the Mother

The submission of the ego is followed by the rebirth in Christ. It is the acceptance of the death of the ego. Becoming one with the Love Light of God the Mother is the next step after the acceptance of the Love Light. It is the acceptance of life.

In the Bible, this is called 'coming to Jesus', or as it says somewhere else in the Bible: 'going through Jesus'. Visions show the face of Jesus as an image that radiates only love and light. When you fully accept and submit yourself to this image of the perfect God-man and the Love Light that shines from Him, the Love Light will enter your own heart. It is the outpouring of the Holy Spirit, the baptism from the Spirit or the baptism in life. At an energetic level, the Love Light of God literally flows from the top of your head into your heart. This is the moment that your heart-awareness opens. You will still regularly fall back into your ego-centred awareness but, from now on, you can always find the opportunity to open your heart-awareness.

Many other religions know this phenomenon as well. For Hindus, it is becoming one with Rama, Krishna, or the guru. Buddhists become one with Buddha. In fact, it is becoming one with the archetypical ideal of the God-man, the acceptance of the fact that you are a God-man yourself, a Son of God. For Jews, Christians, and Muslims, it is the spiritual coming of the Messiah.

We should not think that all people are deprived of the Love Light. This is certainly not the case as the Love Light is equally present in every person. The only difference is that after becoming one with God the Mother, you are aware of the Love Light. It is not something you can achieve by a wilful act. It will happen when you are ready and receptive, and it will feel as mercy being poured out onto you.

Stage 5 Becoming One with God the Father

Becoming one with God the Father is, again, a moment in which you suddenly feel and know who and what you are. It is the moment of 'self-actualisation'. You realise that you are the infinite, unchangeable, eternal truth. You are the Creator of all things. You are one with God the Father. You encompass the entire Creation but there is still a divide between you and Creation. During this stage, there are still antitheses between truth and untruth, form and formlessness, and between you and Creation.

When you have become one with God the Father, you may experience a time of loneliness. God the Father is nothing but emptiness. Besides you, there is no one else. All there is, is emptiness, an endlessly eternal, unchangeable truth.

Stage 6 Becoming One with God the Son

Still, after becoming one with God the Father, the following question arises: 'What about Creation?' Creation comes forth from the Creator. The Creator incorporates Creation and not vice versa. The Creator and Creation, the unchangeable truth and changeable illusions, are two sides of the same coin. One cannot exist without the other. No Creation means no Creator. No Creator means no Creation. It is like this with all antitheses. If there is an 'I', there must be a 'you'; if there is a subject, there must also be an object.

When all antitheses disappear, the identification with the ego ceases to be, there will be no identification with the Love Light, no identification with the formless awareness, and no identification with Creation. There will no longer be good and evil. Only the limitless here and now exists. Creation emerges from the Creator and goes down in it. Life and death merge in Existence. All there is, is what is. There is 'El Jazim'.

You are now what is and what is not, the Creator and the Creation, the form and the formlessness. Heaven and Earth have merged. Light and darkness have merged. There are a new Heaven and a new Earth.

Stage 7 Christ-Awareness

In stage 7, all personal inclinations will slowly disappear. All personal inclinations are founded on the fear of death. If you penetrate deeply into this fear, you will find the solution. That is the moment of understanding that Creation is not real. Creation is maya, an illusion. That's when life and death merge. That's when Muriel reaches the bottom of the bottomless pit and rises from the pit. That is when the new soul transfigures and the rose of the Rosicrucian's turns gold. That is when Gnosis illuminates the soul. That is when the Golden Christ Child is born. You feel no more reason for anger as there is no longer a reason to fear. There is no longer a reason to fear because you are all that is. The eternal, unchangeable reality invulnerable, and the changeable unreality is an illusion that doesn't exist. While this realisation grows, there will come a moment that you are no longer capable of feeling anger or concerns. You are now Christ, the only born Son of God. God the Father, the Love Light of God the Mother, and God the Son have all become one. God, the Love Light, and Creation are what is. You are what is and there is no more space for personal inclinations. You are now living in the Christ-awareness. Nothing else exists but Existence-Consciousness-Bliss.

As the love grows, there will come a moment that love encompasses everything. When all antitheses have gone and there is but one love that encompasses everything, then there is nothing but Love. This love for God will then be equal to the love for yourself. The love for your neighbour will then be equal to the love for yourself, and it will be equal to the love for God. When love encompasses everything, love no longer needs a reference framework so love will actually no longer exist. It is the final inclination of the ego that must be relinquished. It is when you have fully achieved what Jesus commanded: Love God above all else and your neighbour as yourself. Your heart is now an open well that flows without any inhibition. Your love encompasses Creation and blesses everything that enters your awareness.

12

The Growth Pattern Through the Stages of the Path

In this chapter, I describe the growth pattern of the development as it occurs in every stage of the seven stages of the Path to a heart-centred awareness. I added this chapter to create a bridge between development psychology and transpersonal psychology on the one hand, and the religious/spiritual Path to a heart-centred awareness on the other hand. Besides that, the description of the growth pattern through the different stages will allow you to recognise your glories and your fears.

Growth Pattern of Development

The process of going through the seven stages of the Path to a heart-centred awareness follows a fixed pattern that is the same with every stage. The growth pattern of development consists of:

1. Insight/submission
Insight will lead to releasing the identification with a certain self-image and turn into an identification of a higher self-image. You will experience this higher self-image as a wonderful glory.
2. Glory
You cling on to this newly-found glory.
3. Dilemma/fear
You begin to see that your glory is not the highest glory. You are afraid of losing your glory but you also fear the higher self-image that you don't know yet.
4. Growth
You grow towards the moment of gaining new insight, a new

moment of submission, and a new identification at a higher level.

Before you come to faith, you fully identify yourself with your body, your thoughts, and your ego. You are receptive to all ego-based inclinations such as fear, anger, desire, repulsion, and ignorance. The body, your thoughts, and your ego are your glory. You strive for the body, thoughts, and ego to become one. The dilemma is that you start to feel in your heart that there is more than just your ego, but you don't know what it is and, therefore, you fear it.

Development Stage 1 Coming to Faith

Insight/submission
The soul's memory of the oneness with God, from whence it was created, becomes ever stronger and you will reach a point where it is strong enough to enter your consciousness as a bolt of lightning and you know that God exists. This is the 'coming to faith' moment.

Glory
When you have come to faith, you live in the glorious knowledge that God exists, that he is omnipotent, omniscient, and omnipresent, and that he loves you for who and what you are. If you see God in your mind as a person, then God loves you, he knows you, and he protects you. He is your Father in Heaven who is always by your side. He is nothing but good and his love for you is endless.

Dilemma/fear
The dilemma is that you don't know and can't know God. You are separated from God and, moreover, you have created an image of God and this image doesn't match with reality because

it is an antithesis of something else that is utterly evil, the devil. In reality, there are no antitheses but that is still beyond your personal experience. You are afraid to lose God's glorious love and you fear the devil. If you see God as a person, you will also fear God because you can imagine him getting angry with you and punishing you if he wants to.

Growth
Growth is the process that sees your need for God's love and protection slowly decline, which also lessens the fear for the antithesis.

Development Stage 2 Coming to Repentance

Insight/submission
You realise that faith is not enough. You have to live like it and make your faith your first priority.

Glory
Coming to repentance is the final stage before you submit yourself to God. In this final stage, the ego develops to its maximal capacity and into a mature, healthy, and balanced ego in which the body, thoughts, and ego become one. Before you enter this stage, you have already realised that negativity, the urge to destruct, anger, and desire never lead to a feeling of bliss. Your faith is strong and you live your life for God. Now you will try to feel happiness through positivity, by helping others, creativity, giving love, and self-actualisation. You follow the rules of society, and the meaning of your life becomes the meaning that you wish to give it.

Dilemma/fear
Still, this will ultimately not lead to sustainable happiness. You feel that your body, thoughts, and ego are no longer satisfactory

but you are afraid to stop identifying yourself with the ego. The ego has now been fully developed but this will also maximise the fear of death.

Growth
You slowly grow towards the realisation that your ego no longer offers satisfaction and you become less afraid of death.

Development Stage 3 Submission to God and Rebirth in Christ

Insight/submission
You come to realise that you are not the key to everlasting happiness, and you submit yourself completely to God. You can see God as a person or as a being that is everything.

Glory
You are now a servant of God. He is responsible for everything and He will organise and dedicate everything for you. He offers you the here and now that can be nothing other than perfect for you because God loves you.

Dilemma/fear
After your submission, you have been reborn in Christ. You were born again and you are aware of that, but this new 'you' still has to grow and you still mostly identify yourself with your ego. You are haunted by personal inclinations as you were convinced that you had given them up. The new consciousness has just been born and barely has any influence yet. You may not appear changed at all and you don't notice that God is guiding you. You are afraid to take responsibility of your life and you fear life itself.

Growth

Your personal inclinations diminish and so diminishes your fear of life. The realisation grows that you have to live your own life and that God is not doing that for you. You have to assume full responsibility for your life in some way.

Development Stage 4 Becoming One with God the Mother

Insight/submission

And then suddenly, you have a vision and find yourself eye-to-eye with Jesus. Jesus symbolises the highest conceivable God-man. The light that shines from him is almost too bright to bear. This light is the Love Light of God the Mother. You submit yourself to the Love Light, and realise that the Love Light is inside you. God the Mother fills your heart with the Love Light until it overflows.

Glory

You are constantly in the Love Light that fills you up completely and you accept life in all its glory.

Dilemma/fear

You slowly get used to feeling yourself in the Love Light all the time. You even notice it less and less. You're still not perfectly happy and you don't know what to do with yourself. And besides that, you can still feel your personal inclinations pulling at you. How can that be, when you are one with God the Mother? You feel guilty towards God, Moses, Jesus, or Mohammed, who has given you so much love and trust. You are afraid of finding out who your true self is and also of losing the Love Light.

Growth

The realisation that the entire Creation is made of Love Light is growing. Your love for all creatures grows and you wish to share your love with everything and everyone. Your wish to know your true self is growing. You can no longer see God as a person.

Development Stage 5 Becoming One with God the Father

Insight/submission

The question of 'Who am I?' is finally answered and you accept your true self. You are the infinite, everlasting, unchangeable truth. God the Father himself. You no longer identify yourself with the Love Light.

Glory

You feel infinitely great because the entire Creation arises and goes down inside you. You are pure consciousness and eternal. You can never die again.

Dilemma/fear

You may now be the eternal truth but where does this leave the untruth? You are the Creator, but what about Creation? Creation is a strange state that arises inside you and, more importantly, is constantly changing and unreal. Creation and the fact that everything is constantly changing is something you fear. Apart from that, you feel very lonely as there is nothing besides yourself.

Growth

Your fear for Creation and life diminishes. You start to accept that Creation constantly changes and you exist by the grace of Creation. After all, there is no Creation without the Creator.

Development Stage 6 Becoming One with God the Son

Insight/submission

Suddenly, you realise that the Creator and Creation, God the Father and God the Son are two sides of the same coin. You are not just the Creator. You are also Creation and every part of it. Form and formlessness become one. You no longer identify yourself with the emptiness of God the Father. All antitheses have been negated.

Glory

Now you are everything there is. You are no longer in the here and now, you have become the here and now. You are life itself. There is perception and this fills you up with joy. The highest conception of God. God is 'I am' is now your truth.

Dilemma/fear

You still identify yourself with your ego, albeit minimally, and you are still receptive to the ego's inclinations. You still feel some desire and anger.

You are afraid to let go of your ego and its inclinations altogether.

Growth

The identification with your ego gradually diminishes and its inclinations wear off too. The moments that you still feel anger create an intolerable tension within yourself, although this happens less and less often. You feel a calm sense of peace descend upon you, and your emotions dwindle. Your heart, however, overflows with love for what is.

Development Stage 7 Coming to Christ-Awareness

Insight/submission

You realise that every personal inclination goes against your will, against the will of God, and you no longer identify yourself with your ego and its inclinations. You also relinquish the identification with the Love Light of God the Mother, and with the emptiness of the Father and the comprehensiveness of Creation. Yet there is still fear, and therefore the inclinations of the ego have not completely disappeared. The last insight is that you realise that Creation is not reality. If Creation is not real, nothing can harm you anymore.

Glory

Existence is a glory, but you even don't feel any connection with that. Dilemmas and fear are completely of the past. The highest understanding of God and the highest understanding of love have lost their meaning. You have returned to the natural state of Existence-Consciousness-Bliss. You are now completely living in the Christ-awareness.

13

Practical Instructions to Follow the Path

The previous chapters described the seven development stages you can go through to go from an ego-centred awareness to a heart-centred awareness. In this chapter, I will offer some practical tips that can be used if you wish to embark on this journey. These tips, or pieces of advice, add to the information that has already been described in chapter 10 The Path to a Heart-Centred Awareness.

Praying, Singing, Coming Together

You can stimulate your growth in love and awareness by praying, singing, and coming together. This is all about the process of creation. You were created as a human being, so you are part of the Creation, and thus a Son of God. It also makes you one with God. You were created in the image of God the Father. That means that you, like God the Father, have the capability to create and that the Love Light from which your creations are made flows from you, from your heart.

All of your thoughts are your creation. All of your thoughts are made of the Love Light. In reality, God is indivisible. There is but one God, one Love Light, and one Creation. As soon as your thought arises, all the Love Light that is part of Creation vibrates with your thought as long as the thought is based on the love in your heart. The stronger you believe that your thought becomes reality, the likelier the chance that your thought will actually manifest itself in the tangible world.

The Bible says the following:

And when they came to the crowd, a man came up to him and, kneeling before him, he said, 'Lord, have mercy on my son, for he

> *is an epileptic and he suffers terribly. For often he falls into the fire, and often into the water. And I brought him to your disciples, and they could not heal him.' And Jesus answered, 'O faithless and twisted generation, how long am I to be with you? How long am I to bear with you? Bring him here to me.' And Jesus rebuked the demon, and it came out of him, and the boy was healed instantly. Then the disciples came to Jesus privately and said, 'Why could we not cast it out?' He said to them, 'Because of your little faith. For truly, I say to you, if you have faith like a grain of mustard seed, you will say to this mountain, "Move from here to there," and it will move, and nothing will be impossible for you. But this kind is only cast out by prayer and fasting.'*
> (Matthew 17:14-21)

A thought is a creation, and the stronger the belief that the thought will come true, the bigger the chance that this will truly happen. When your faith is strong enough, which is: as big as a grain of mustard, then your thought will move so much Love Light that it will move a mountain. When you pray that you will continue to grow in the Love Light and you thank God for your growth and the mercy that he pours out upon you ceaselessly, then you will also grow in the Love Light. Singing and praying are forms of creation and a hugely stimulating force for opening the heart energy. Being together with others who share your thoughts will strengthen the process of creation. When you and a hundred other people are in a church, praying to God, then this empowers the force that will make your prayer manifest itself.

However, creating something with our ego-centred will is not very effective. The ego is constantly torn between different thoughts and emotions, and the awareness that forms the foundation of all elements of Creation will not vibrate along with your will because your will is not consistent. The creative force can only come from your heart, when your desire truly comes from your soul without the interference of the ego. When you let go of everything and you accept Creation for what it is, a creative development in line with what you truly wish in your heart will be the result. Praying, singing, and coming together are a good way to help your growth, but only when it comes from the heart.

Nutrition

Your physical condition is partly determined by what you eat. Healthy foodstuffs are fruits, vegetables, nuts, seeds, and grain. All other foodstuffs are unhealthy. I advise you to follow a vegetarian diet, so no meat and no fish. The main reason for this is the connection you make with animal energies when you eat meat or fish. Apart from that, eating meat is simply unhealthy and bad for the environment. And let's not forget that animals, after mankind, are the most developed creatures on Earth. Animals are your brothers. They are also God's creatures. They can experience pain and feel emotions. We are commanded to love all creatures and that includes animals. Exploiting and killing animals for pleasure is everything but loving.

You need to make sure that you get enough Vitamin B12, iodine, and zinc when you eat a vegetarian diet for a longer time. If necessary, you can take some supplements to make sure that you do. You eat to feed yourself but we also eat because it gives us pleasure. So don't forget to enjoy your food, even when the thing you eat is not healthy. So if now and then you eat something unhealthy don't feel guilty, but enjoy it.

Breathing

One of the conditions for spiritual growth is a mature and stable, fully developed ego. Before spiritual growth, there is psychological growth. Your ego tends to stow away unprocessed emotions or emotions you don't allow yourself to feel in the so-called subconsciousness, which roots energetically in your abdomen. Deep abdominal breathing helps to dislodge these energies when you consciously follow your breathing. Breathe in and send your breath first to your lower back, then to your anus, then to your genitals, and to your pubic bone, and then via your navel upwards to your chest. By doing this, you first fill up your lower abdomen from behind and from below, then from the front, and then upwards. This is how you relax all the muscles in your lower abdomen and you can release all your suppressed emotions. Just keep practising this until it becomes second nature, which may take years but it is certainly worth it. Apart from that, bottled-up emotions also often lead to unnecessary muscle tension. That is why letting go of these emotions consciously really helps. Such a tension can be released by relaxing the muscles of the jaw, by relaxing and dropping the shoulders, and by relaxing the pectoral, abdominal, and pelvic muscles.

Dedication

You may have come to faith and repentance, but the next step to submitting yourself totally to God is a huge step that only few people take. When you submit yourself to God, you accept the death of your ego and put your trust in God. A method that helps to achieve that is by submitting yourself to God over and over again. Pray: 'Father, not my will but yours be done.' Kneel if you want to and submit yourself to God. Again and again.

Letting Go

Still, after submitting yourself to God and the rebirth in Christ that follows, the ego is not yet gone. You still have thoughts and emotions and you still feel attached to many things of which you were not even aware. Let go of everything. Let go of your past, your future, your fears, your anger, your sadness, the emotional ties with your loved ones, your possessions, everything. You don't need to give everything away or break with people. It's all about putting everything in the hands of God. Let go of everything you feel emotionally attached to and offer it to God. That is letting go.

Neti Neti

A specific Hindu method can also be used to facilitate the transfer to stage 5 Becoming one with God the Father. This method is called 'Neti neti', which means 'not this, not this'. The transfer to stage 5 is also called the step to self-actualisation. It is the moment you realise who you truly are. You can experience who you truly are when you ask God the question, 'Who am I?' When you ask this question and pray for an answer and you ask this question with all your might and energy because wanting to know who you are is absolutely all you wish to know, then God will let you experience who you are through his mercy. Unfortunately, this is easier said than done. Most people have to be satisfied with little steps and that is what the neti neti method is used for. Ask yourself who you are and say with every answer you can think off: 'Neti neti.' 'Not this, not this.' Whatever you can think of, that is not you. Keep doing this until there is nothing left but the empty void that is God the Father. Acknowledge that you are this empty void.

Tat Tvam Asi

Another Hindu method can be used to facilitate the transfer to stage 6 Becoming one with God the Son. This method is contrary to 'neti neti' and is called 'Tat tvam asi'. This means 'I am that'. When you have come to self-actualisation for the first time and you are now one with the Father, the infinite, unchangeable, eternal truth, you are still not one with Creation. To negate that separation and realise that 'you' are 'that', you can say to yourself: 'Tat tvam asi.' 'I am that.' It is mostly very useful if you feel anger or fear something, or when you have other negative emotions.

14

Meditation Exercises

Meditating regularly is basically essential for spiritual growth. I recommend that you meditate at least once a day for at least 15 minutes by using the following practical instructions. Sit down in a relaxed position with a straight back. You can assume a half or full lotus position, either on the floor or on a cushion. You can also sit on a meditation stool and sit with your lower legs folded under the stool, or on a meditation cushion with your legs on both sides. You can even use a regular chair if that's more comfortable for you. Breathe in by using the breathing technique as described above. Breathe in slowly through your nose, and breathe out through your mouth. When you feel yourself becoming more relaxed and quieter, breathe out through your nose as well. Keep your hands on top of each other, on your lower abdomen, with both palms of your hands upwards and the tips of your thumbs against each other. You can also put your hands on your thighs, again with the palms of your hands up or down, whatever you find most comfortable. Keep this position for a few minutes and relax your muscles as much as you can. Lower the rhythm of your breathing until you are completely relaxed. This is the concentration phase. Focus on your breathing and on relaxing your muscles. You can close your eyes or keep them half open without focusing on your environment. You will notice that you still have thoughts going through your mind. The art of meditation is to reach a state that you no longer follow and hold on to your thoughts, but you let them go until all your thoughts have left you. It will take time and practice to achieve this. Still, between your different thoughts, you may recognise a moment of having no thoughts. Try to stay in this moment. The more you practise, the longer you will manage to stay in that moment until the moment lasts without having any thoughts. You are now floating around in the here and now, so to speak, and without having any thoughts. The only thing there is, is consciousness. This is the meditation phase.

You can add a phase of contemplation between the concentration phase and the meditation phase. Contemplation means that you consider a particular theme. You can use the contemplation phase to do a specific exercise that can be part of the spiritual development phase you are in. Below, you can find some specific exercises for the stages 3 to 6.

Contemplation exercise for stage 3 Submission and Rebirth in Christ

Visualise the image you have of your God. Feel the unconditional Love of God and see how God's Love shines from him as a radiating Light that totally encompasses you. Submit yourself to God. Submit yourself totally to God and put everything in his hands. Let go of your future and your past and put them in God's hands. Put all your desires, your will, your anger, your guilt, your hatred, and your fear in God's hands. Submit everything you feel attached to and put it all in God's hands. Be perfectly happy with the here and now because this is the moment that God has granted you. Stay in this moment of submission and then enter the meditation phase.

Contemplation exercise for stage 4 Becoming one with God the Mother

Visualise the image you have of your God, of Jesus, or of the perfect God-man. Feel the unconditional Love of God and see how God's Love shines from him as a radiating Light that totally encompasses you. Feel how your body fully dissolves in the Love Light that shines from God. You are now a Love Light body. Approach God and merge with the Love Light of God that you just summoned for yourself. The source of this Love Light is your heart. Stay in this Love Light of God and then enter the meditation phase.

Contemplation exercise for stage 5 Becoming one with God the Father

Visualise the image you have of the infinite, unchangeable, eternal truth. Imagine what it feels like to be this infinite, unchangeable, eternal truth. Let it expand until it fully encompasses you and become one with it. You are now the infinite, unchangeable, eternal truth. This is a total emptiness and you encompass all there is. You are now one with God the Father, the source of Creation. Stay in this moment and then enter the meditation phase.

Contemplation exercise for stage 6 Becoming one with God the Son

You are the infinite, unchangeable, eternal truth. You are God the Father, the Creator. Feel how the Love Light of God the Mother flows from you and feeds and encompasses the whole of Creation. You are the Creator, but there can be no Creator without Creation. The Creation has come from you and is entirely made of the Love Light. You have become one with Creation. You are the Creation. Feel how all the antitheses between Creator and Creation have disappeared. Feel how all the antitheses between you and God have disappeared. Feel how all the antitheses merge until God the Father, the Love Light of God the Mother, and Creation are one. This is what you are, but you no longer exist, there is only what is. This is the state of Existence-Consciousness-Bliss. Stay in this moment and then enter the meditation phase.

15

Baptism

The following few chapters are about several Christian doctrines that most people are only able to understand when they know more about the development path to the heart-centred awareness. This first chapter is about the ritual of baptism.

The Bible mentions several baptisms, which is why it may seem that there are different types of baptism. Some people believe that there are five different baptisms while others think there are even more. When we compare the baptisms to the seven development stages, it becomes clear that Christianity observes three baptisms that confirm the first four development stages.

1. Baptism with water as a confirmation of coming to faith and repentance.
This baptism is offered to everyone who did not believe but came to faith. This form of baptism is given to Jews (who are circumcised) and gentiles (who are not circumcised).
2. Baptism with water confirms the rebirth in Christ.
It is also called the baptism into death as the submission to God hails the start of the death of the ego. At the same time, it is the birth in Christ or in the heart-centred awareness.
3. Baptism with the Holy Spirit.
This is also called the baptism with the Spirit or fire, or the baptism into life, thus confirming the pouring out of the Holy Spirit or the newly established unity with the Love Light of God.

Below, you can find some Bible entries that relate to these different types of baptism.

I baptise you with water for repentance (first baptism), *but he who is coming after me is mightier than I, whose sandals I am not worthy to carry. He will baptise you with the Holy Spirit and fire* (third baptism).
(Matthew 3:11 and similarly, John 1:31)

We were buried therefore with him by baptism into death (second baptism), *in order that, just as Christ was raised from the dead by the glory of the Father, we too might walk in newness of life* (rebirth in the Christ-awareness).
(Romans 6:4)

For in one Spirit, we were all baptised into one body—Jews or Greeks, slaves or free—and all were made to drink of one Spirit (third baptism, the pouring out of the Holy Spirit).
(1 Corinthians 12:13)

For in him the whole fullness of deity dwells bodily, and you have been filled in him (third baptism), *who is the head of all rule and authority. In him also you were circumcised with a circumcision made without hands, by putting off the body of the flesh, by the circumcision of Christ* (third baptism). *Having been buried with him in baptism* (second baptism), *in which you were also raised with him* (third baptism) *through faith in the powerful working of God, who raised him from the dead.*
(Colossians 2:9-12)

While Peter was still saying these things, the Holy Spirit fell on all who heard the word (third baptism). *And the believers from among the circumcised who had come with Peter were amazed, because the gift of the Holy Spirit was poured out even on the Gentiles. For they were hearing them speaking in tongues and extolling God. Then Peter declared, 'Can anyone withhold water for baptising these people, who have received the Holy Spirit just*

as we have?' And he commanded them to be baptised in the name of Jesus Christ (first or second baptism).
(Acts 10:44-48)

In this part, Peter explains that when the Holy Spirit comes down on someone, then this person cannot be refused baptism by water to symbolise rebirth in Christ because the pouring out of the Holy Spirit is the next phase after the rebirth in Christ. That these people are gentiles, meaning not Jewish, is irrelevant.

The baptism does not affect your development and it doesn't wash away your sins. It is also not possible to move on from being a descendent of Adam to becoming a descendent of Christ. This can only be realised by submitting yourself to God and being reborn in Christ, which is the transfer of the ego-centred awareness to the heart-centred awareness.

Many Christian churches baptise children. This baptism, however, doesn't confirm the coming to repentance or the rebirth in Christ. By having their child baptised, the parents confirm that they will raise the child according to Christian morals and teachings, and that they let the child enter the union between God and Abraham. People say that Jews enter the union between God and Abraham through circumcision, like the way Christians do this through baptism.

Whatever people say about baptism, it is a ritual. Rituals can be an instrument but that is all they are. The act of being baptised does not induce a person's development but it can confirm a specific development stage.

Baptisms are generally confirmed by the words:

I baptise you in the name of the Father, of the Son, and of the Holy Spirit.

These words are based on what Jesus commanded:

Therefore, go and make disciples of all nations, baptizing them in the name of the Father and of the Son and of the Holy Spirit... (Matthew 28:19)

Jesus did not say:

Go and judge the people and only when you deem them worthy, you shall baptise them in the name of the Father, of the Son, and of the Holy Spirit.

The commandment given by Jesus means that every person may baptise another person and that everyone is entitled to being baptised. Every person who wishes to confirm a certain development stage has the right to be baptised, meaning also Jews and Muslims.

Some churches baptise by sprinkling a bit of water onto the person's head, other churches have a full submersion ritual, and this is a strongly debated issue. But when you understand the symbolism of baptism, the debate is totally unnecessary.

The first baptism, as a confirmation of coming to faith and repentance, can be done by sprinkling water because the person who is baptised has not yet submersed themselves in anything. The second baptism symbolises the submersion in death, so in my opinion, this baptism would best be done by submersion in water. However, there are not many people who truly submit themselves fully to God and are thus reborn in Christ.

The just-quoted commandment given by Jesus to baptise starts with the words:

Go and make disciples of all nations...

For the Christian churches, this is the foundation for evangelicalism and it has led to the fact that there are now around 1.2 billion Christians in the world. This commandment has fulfilled an important function although this function has mostly lost its meaning in this day and age, insofar it is interpreted literally.

The danger that lies in this message is that people and church communities believe that it gives them a certain authority based on which they will then evangelise others from their ego-centred awareness with their ego-centred will. But that has never been the intention behind the commandment. It is good to spread light and love across the world. It is good to spread the message of Love as Christ taught us across the world, also among other peoples. But it is not a call to convert the entire world population and make them Christians. You can find the difference by listening closely to your heart. Try to live from your heart-centred awareness, and when your heart tells you to spread light and love, then please do, but always with respect for the other person and their cultural and religious background.

Finally Jesus said:

> *... baptizing them in the name of the Father and of the Son and of the Holy Spirit.*

The name of the Father and of the Son and of the Holy Spirit is El Jazim. So baptise everyone who says 'yes' to God in the name El Jazim.

16

Original Sin and Reconciliation

Important doctrines in Christian churches are the fall of man, the original sin, the aspect of reconciliation, and the belief that Jesus died for your sins.

The fall of man symbolises the souls getting separated from God because they started to individualise, follow their own will, and live their lives from an ego-centred awareness. In truth, it is impossible to separate yourself from God, but you can create an illusion of separation through your thoughts, emotions, and judgements. This is symbolically described as Adam and Eve having eaten from the Tree of knowledge of good and evil after which they were expelled from paradise. Having knowledge of good and evil means having knowledge of antitheses. This knowledge of antitheses can only be negated in stage 6 Becoming one with God the Son, with Creation. That is when Adam and Eve return to paradise and the separation between the antitheses and between man and God is lifted. It is also the moment that a person has fully transferred from an ego-centred awareness to a heart-centred awareness, although there will still be some personal inclinations.

The consequence of the fall of man is the original sin. Every person who is born is deemed sinful automatically because the soul is sinful. The sin is that you follow your personal, ego-centred inclinations and you fail to turn to God. Only when you 'turn around', meaning the moment you submit yourself to God and you are reborn in Christ, you are no longer a sinful person and you start your reconciliation with God. It is the moment that the angels turn around on Jacob's ladder and ascend back to heaven. The fall of man has turned into a return to God.

Jesus dying on the cross symbolises the death of the ego and the consequential rebirth in Christ. This is the moment when the heart-centred awareness awakens. So it doesn't mean that, by dying on the cross, Jesus took your sins upon himself. You will have to die to your ego by submitting yourself to God.

The word 'sin' has a negative connotation. Sin implies that you are a bad person. But sin, in relation with the fall of man and the original sin, is not bad. It is the natural development of the soul to go through the ego-centred phase. Only through experiencing this ego-centred phase and the suffering it brings, can a person grow towards the heart-centred awareness.

17

Suffering

Saying 'Yes' is what causes bliss. Saying 'no' is what causes suffering.

Suffering is a difficult subject. Saying to someone who suffers that the cause of their suffering is not what they say 'no' to, but the fact that they say 'no', is rather heartless because you deny that this person is suffering and you blame them for their suffering. But it is still what I say to you now. I'm not saying it because I deny the reason for your suffering. I'm saying it to offer you a way out of your suffering.

Saying 'no' can be caused by three things:

1. You are not receiving what you want.
2. You receive what you don't want.
3. Ignorance.

The solution for your suffering is simple yet very difficult at the same time: say 'yes'. Saying 'yes' means letting go of your ego-centred awareness and love everything that enters your awareness with all your heart. Living from a heart-centred awareness is your natural state. There is only Existence-Consciousness-Bliss and no more suffering. When you are not ready to do this, then keep faith. Love is preceded by faith. Faith is the foundation for saying 'yes'. Faith means that, despite your ignorance, you still believe that what happens to you happens for a reason and is good as it is. No matter how difficult.

When another person is suffering, you will not help him by pointing out the true cause of his suffering. You can only help and support him. You can be there for him. You can love him and say 'yes' to him. You often suffer as well. And still, God says 'yes' to you, always. Have faith in God and say 'yes' yourself. Say 'yes' to those who are near you and suffer, and love them.

18

Reincarnation, Karma, and Redemption

Reincarnation is the process whereby a soul expresses itself in the lives of successively born people. The soul gains experiences through the lives that these people live, the choices they make, and the consequences of these choices.

The concept of reincarnation only gets its specific meaning when time is experienced as a reality. In the higher stages of spiritual development, all antitheses come together, and only the here and now remains while the illusion of time and space fades away. From the awareness in these higher stages, time is an illusion and so is reincarnation. Every step in the development process must be taken in the here and now in order to be effective. Growth always happens now. The only reason that we perceive that growth is because there is the illusion of time. So from the perspective of unity, reincarnation doesn't exist.

Reincarnation is not included in the Jewish, Christian, and Islamic holy scriptures. It's not taught but its existence is also not denied. It is simply not mentioned. Reincarnation is, however, a subject within the esoteric schools of Judaism, Christianity, and Islam. That is why believing in reincarnation doesn't go against the Jewish, Christian, or Islamic faiths.

Reincarnation also doesn't exist from the perspective of the ego as the ego is an integrated part of your body, your emotions, and your thoughts. When you die, the ego dies as well and it cannot be born again. However, as a person, you may still be affected by reincarnation because your soul went through certain experiences in the past lives of other people with whom your soul was connected. The consequences of how these people acted, and their experiences, will have an impact on your life.

Let me first explain more about the process of creation so

it may be easier to understand. The soul is created by God. Imagine God as a large, empty sphere. This large sphere creates something: a soul, depicted as a little sphere. When the large sphere creates a little sphere, then the little sphere can never be created outside the large sphere. After all, there is nothing apart from God, so there is nothing apart from the large sphere. So the little sphere is created within the large sphere. The Creation, the little sphere, is inside the Creator, the large sphere. The little sphere is also made of the same substance of which the large sphere is made of as there is no other substance. To sum it up, the little sphere is created by the large sphere, inside the large sphere and consisting of the same substance as the large sphere. When the little sphere dies, it returns to its origin, the large sphere, and all the substance the little sphere was created from returns to its original state.

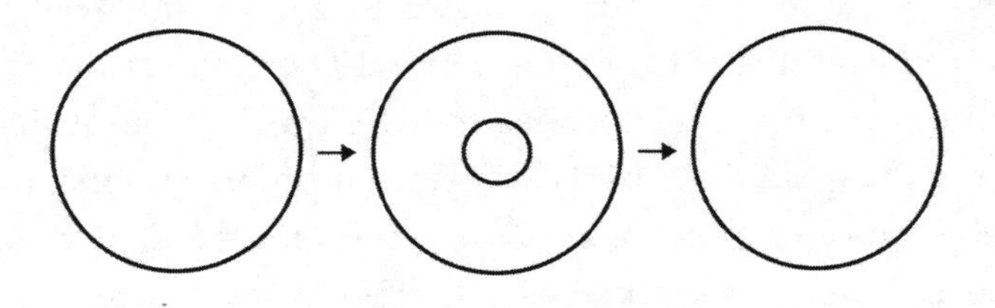

Figure 6. God, Creation, God

The little sphere is the soul. The soul is created from God the Father, and when it dies, it becomes one with God the Father again. The substance of which everything exists is the Love Light of God the Mother. The Love Light of God the Mother is the God-substance. Your soul, that which you truly are, is created by God. God is perfect and so your soul, which is you, is perfect too.

There are no antitheses in God and all is one. That means that you are entirely one with God and, like God, you have the ability to create. Every thought you have can be seen as a creation. When you create a thought, it consists of the Love

Light. When your thought dies because it is no longer nurtured by you, your thought, your creation, returns to the source from where it came. If a thought is strong enough, it can manifest itself in the material reality. And because every creation ultimately returns to its source, you, as the creator of your creation, bear the consequences of this creation. That is karma.

The consequence of this all is that you will constantly be experiencing circumstances in your life that 1) are the result of the past and everything that happened in that past, and 2) are created by your soul without you being aware of this. These circumstances happen to you and there is nothing you can do about them. But you do have a choice of how you deal with them. You can say 'yes' and accept your circumstances and make the best of them, or you can say 'no' and fight your circumstances. You will be happy when you say 'yes' and unhappy when you say 'no'.

Creation itself is a creative process. Something is created out of nothing. You don't have to do anything to make that happen. People living from their ego-centred awareness tend to say 'no', after which they want to create something by exerting their will. They send a beam of energy from the centre of their willpower, the solar plexus, trying to change Creation and make something happen. This may work for a while, but most often it doesn't because your will is directed by your ego, which is driven by different and often contradicting impulses. For example, you want something but, at the same time, you have doubts. You want something but, at the same time, you are afraid. This will not induce the process of creation.

When you live from your heart-centred awareness, you accept life as it comes. You open your heart and say 'yes' and Creation can take its own creative course. The will then becomes subordinate to the wishes of your heart. When you wish to create something with your heart, without any influence from the ego, then the energy of the will shall conform to what the heart wants and the flow of creative energy will join your heart. When this happens, the entire Creation and all the consciousness on which it is based will follow the heart's vibrations, and what you wish for will be created. This means that you can create your own reality but not from the ego-centred will. Even if you do manage to create something with your ego-centred will, it usually will be a temporary, enforced state that will not last for long.

The process of rebirth, whereby a soul is constantly gaining new experiences by merging itself with a next person, is called the 'cycle of rebirth'. It is possible to liberate yourself from this cycle of rebirth and it doesn't require following all the seven stages of the Path to the heart-centred awareness. It can be done quicker.

I already explained that you are not a person and not your ego, but that you are your soul. But this is not all there is to it. Your soul has come into existence at some point. It is created by the will and the desire of God the Father. It is energy that has become denser than the formless ocean of energy that is God the Mother. Some level of individuality was created which distinguished itself from the rest. Your soul has gained experiences and so you can imagine your soul as a collection of all those experiences. This means that the soul is not something static. It changes as it gains experiences. Now that the soul is born and changing, it has become part of Creation. Creation can only be identified by something that doesn't change. Change can only be perceived by something that doesn't change. This something that doesn't change is exactly what you truly are. You are a sliver of God-awareness. It is the core of your heart. It is a spark of God's awareness in which the entire Creation arises and goes down again. It is so close to you that, most of the time, you don't see it, but it is very simple. It is your own awareness. And it is this awareness, this Divine core, that is entirely one with all awareness. In reality, there is only one awareness and that is the awareness of God. That is why the Messiah can say:

Your heart and my heart, is one heart, it's the heart of all, it's the heart of God.

And that is why God can say:

I am your life and you are my consciousness.

And that is why the essence of God is: 'Existence-Consciousness-Bliss'.

The moment you realise and truly experience that you are this consciousness, and that Creation arises and goes down again in you, you have the key to your redemption in your hand.

The problem is that you still fall for the tricks of the ego. They are the instruments the ego uses to avoid entering the state of Existence-Consciousness-Bliss. These instruments are:

- Exerting power
- Thoughts, emotions, judgements
- Seeking happiness in external circumstances

The solution is to be aware in the here and now, without any thoughts or emotions, just letting be what is. And when thoughts, emotions, or judgements enter your awareness, you can just consider them as an observer. You can embrace them, love them, feel them, and then let them go. This is very hard at first as the flow of thoughts seems endless, but when you are steadfast in your efforts, the flow of thoughts will diminish and you will find gaps between the thoughts.

Only after death will it become clear whether you have been redeemed from the cycle of rebirth. When you let yourself slide away in your thoughts and emotions after death, then they will keep you hostage and you must certainly reincarnate. If you can stay in the moment of witnessing, of observing, and you are consciously present in the here and now, then there will be space to behold the Love Light of God. Then you can become one with this Love Light.

This is not the end; you still need to evaluate and process your life, and when you have done that, you can be reborn again or you can choose not to. You will be free to choose which experiences you will gain. This can also be in a different star system or universe. You will be redeemed and no longer have to go through the stage of ego-centred awareness.

19

Cain and Abel

Adam and Eve were created in the image of God, but if their children had also been created in the image of God there would never have been renewal. Adam and Eve had three children, Cain, Abel, and Set, who were not created in the image of God.

Cain became a farmer. He cultivated the land. Abel became a shepherd. He didn't create anything new. He tended the sheep and watched. Cain is that part of us that creates. Cain represents the masculine aspect of God, as well as the masculine aspect in each of us. Abel represents the feminine aspect of God, as well as the feminine aspect within each of us. Abel is the Love-Light of God.

When Cain and Abel each made an offering to God, God noted Abel's offering, but he did not notice Cain's offering. Cain became enraged and killed Abel. The blood of Abel cried out from the Earth to God and God cursed Cain. He marked Cain so that he could no longer die, and from then on, Cain had to wander the Earth, without the land he cultivated yielding anything to him.

It is often thought that Abel is good and Cain is bad. That is not true. Without Cain there is no creation and no renewal. We are all Cain. We create, but our creations yield nothing. We wander the Earth and we create, but we are always left unsatisfied. We cannot die because we are marked by God, and so we live life after life and we try to create and seek satisfaction again and again, but we fail.

There is nothing wrong with Cain. The problem is he killed Abel. Every moment of the day, with every thought we have, we kill Abel. We must stop that. Instead of killing Abel, we can love him and let him live. This means we have to lay love at the foundation of everything we think and do, or everything we create. If we unite Cain and Abel in ourselves, then the curse of God will come to an end. Then the land we cultivate will yield a lot. Then the blood of Abel will no longer cry out of the Earth to God and then the Love Light of God with which we create will take its natural place in things.

We are developing from an ego-centred awareness to a heart-centred awareness. If we live from our heart, then we live with love. Then we unite Cain and Abel, and we will create just as God created us. Then our creations will bear fruit and God will notice our offerings because they are filled with love. Then we can die in peace and we can escape our wandering on Earth. Then the wheel of rebirth comes to an end and we return to our original state of Existence-Consciousness-Bliss.

20

The Bride of Christ Doctrine

The Bride of Christ doctrine is not mentioned in the Bible. The Bible does speak about marriage, the bride and the groom several times, sometimes with a symbolic meaning. That is why there is not one Bride doctrine and there is the risk that different passages in the Bible where the terms bride, groom, or marriage are used symbolically are seen as one Bride of Christ doctrine. Below, I will give two well-known examples of where 'bride' is used symbolically but with different meanings.

1 The Bride Who Awaits Her Jesus as Her Groom

The parable of the foolish and wise virgins
At that time, the kingdom of heaven will be like ten virgins who took their lamps and went out to meet the bridegroom. Five of them were foolish and five were wise. The foolish ones took their lamps but did not take any oil with them. The wise ones, however, took oil in jars along with their lamps. The bridegroom was a long time in coming, and they all became drowsy and fell asleep. At midnight, the cry rang out: 'Here's the bridegroom! Come out to meet him!' Then all the virgins woke up and trimmed their lamps. The foolish ones said to the wise, 'Give us some of your oil; our lamps are going out.' 'No,' they replied, 'there may not be enough for both us and you. Instead, go to those who sell oil and buy some for yourselves.' But while they were on their way to buy the oil, the bridegroom arrived. The virgins who were ready went in with him to the wedding banquet. And the door was shut. Later the others also came. 'Lord, Lord,' they said, 'open the door for us!' But he replied, 'Truly I tell you, I don't know you.' Therefore, keep watch,

> *because you do not know the day or the hour.*
> (Matthew 25:1-13)

Similarly, Paul says:

> *I am jealous for you with a godly jealousy. I promised you to one husband, to Christ, so that I might present you as a pure virgin to him.*
> (2 Corinthians 11:2)

These parts are about brides who await the groom. Naturally, the brides are virgins. They are innocents and have not yet had intercourse with the groom. You are the bride. You can be the bride. Everyone can be the bride. Everyone is created by God. So everyone is a child of God. Everyone, in their heart, is Christ the only born Son of God. Regardless of your gender, you are the Son of God. And so is the bride. You are the bride, whether you are a woman, a man, or a transgender person, virgin or no virgin, but you first have to become 'innocent', which means that you have to be reborn in Christ by submitting yourself to God. You will have atoned and you are now a bride who awaits her groom, Jesus Christ.

When the groom arrives, meaning when you look into Jesus' eyes and you become one with the Love Light of God the Mother, you will experience a form of spiritual 'intercourse' with Christ. This is the spiritual marriage with the groom, symbolising stage 4 Becoming one with the Love Light of God the Mother.

2 The Bride Symbolising Paradise

In the Book of Revelation, the bride is used to symbolise paradise, the Kingdom of God, the new Jerusalem, the new heaven, and the new Earth where all antitheses fall away.

> *'Hallelujah! For our Lord God Almighty reigns. Let us rejoice and*

be glad and give him glory! For the wedding of the Lamb has come, and his bride has made herself ready. (Fine linen, bright and clean, was given her to wear; fine linen stands for the righteous acts of God's holy people.)' Then the angel said to me, 'Write this: Blessed are those who are invited to the wedding supper of the Lamb!' And he added, 'These are the true words of God.'
(Book of Revelation 19:7-9)

Then I saw a new heaven and a new earth, or the first heaven and the first earth had passed away, and there was no longer any sea. I saw the Holy City, the new Jerusalem, coming down out of heaven from God, prepared as a bride beautifully dressed for her husband.
(Book of Revelation 21:1-2)

He said to me: 'It is done. I am the Alpha and the Omega, the Beginning and the End. To the thirsty I will give water without cost from the spring of the water of life.'
(Book of Revelation 21:6)

One of the seven angels who had the seven bowls full of the seven last plagues came and said to me, 'Come, I will show you the bride, the wife of the Lamb.' And he carried me away in the Spirit to a mountain great and high, and showed me the Holy City, Jerusalem, coming down out of heaven from God.
(Book of Revelation 21:9-10)

The Spirit and the bride say, 'Come!' And let the one who hears say, 'Come!' Let the one who is thirsty come; and let the one who wishes take the free gift of the water of life.
(Book of Revelation 22:17)

The lamb symbolises Jesus and yourself when you have become one with Jesus. The bride has made herself ready, paradise awaits you.

And God said: 'I am the Alpha and the Omega, the Beginning and the End.' Everything comes from God and returns to God and whoever returns can freely drink from God who offers Life.

This God is God the Father, the Creator, from which everything comes forth and to which everything shall return. The Life is the Love Light of God the Mother of which you are and the entire Creation is made. The Love Light of God shines in your heart when you come to the heart-centred awareness. It is at your disposal because you have accepted it. From a very high mountain, you will see the Holy city of Jerusalem descend from God and from heaven.

And the Love Light and the bride are calling you. 'Come, beloved, come!' And let everyone of you who hears say: 'Come!' All you have to say is: 'Come!' Everyone can say: 'Come, beloved, come!' The sea has disappeared. Death in which you submersed when you submitted yourself to God has passed. You have accepted life and are now one with the Lamb and then with God himself, and now the new Jerusalem, the new heaven, and the new earth descend from God. 'Come, beloved, come! You are so thirsty. The water of life is for you.' You only need to accept it and your thirst will be quenched. You can take it, it is free, it costs nothing. 'Come, beloved, come, take the free gift of the water of life.'

21

The Core Message

Beloved reader,

You are created by God saying Yes, and by saying Yes, God confirms that you are perfect as you are. God saying Yes is his grace that he pours out upon you unfalteringly.

Whoever says 'yes' will be happy. Whoever says 'no' will be unhappy. So open your heart and say 'yes'.

Say 'yes' to God, to life, and to yourself. Say 'yes' to the future, to the past, and to the here and now. Say 'yes' to the ones you love and everyone else. Say 'yes'.

In the name of God,
I bless you with the Love Light of God.
May the Love Light of God
heal and redeem you.
May the Love Light of God
fill your heart until it overflows.
May the Love Light of God be with you,
now and in all eternity.
Amen

Go with God

O-BOOKS

SPIRITUALITY

O is a symbol of the world, of oneness and unity; this eye represents knowledge and insight. We publish titles on general spirituality and living a spiritual life. We aim to inform and help you on your own journey in this life.

If you have enjoyed this book, why not tell other readers by posting a review on your preferred book site?

The Holy Spirit's Interpretation of the New Testament

A Course in Understanding and Acceptance

Regina Dawn Akers

Following on from the strength of *A Course In Miracles*, NTI teaches us how to experience the love and oneness of God.

Paperback: 978-1-84694-085-9 ebook: 978-1-78099-083-5

The Message of A Course In Miracles

A translation of the Text in plain language

Elizabeth A. Cronkhite

A translation of *A Course in Miracles* into plain, everyday language for anyone seeking inner peace. The companion volume, *Practicing A Course In Miracles*, offers practical lessons and mentoring.

Paperback: 978-1-84694-319-5 ebook: 978-1-84694-642-4

Your Simple Path

Find Happiness in every step

Ian Tucker

A guide to helping us reconnect with what is really important in our lives.

Paperback: 978-1-78279-349-6 ebook: 978-1-78279-348-9

365 Days of Wisdom

Daily Messages To Inspire You Through The Year

Dadi Janki

Daily messages which cool the mind, warm the heart and guide you along your journey.

Paperback: 978-1-84694-863-3 ebook: 978-1-84694-864-0

Body of Wisdom

Women's Spiritual Power and How it Serves

Hilary Hart

Bringing together the dreams and experiences of women across the world with today's most visionary spiritual teachers.

Paperback: 978-1-78099-696-7 ebook: 978-1-78099-695-0

Dying to Be Free

From Enforced Secrecy to Near Death to True Transformation

Hannah Robinson

After an unexpected accident and near-death experience, Hannah Robinson found herself radically transforming her life, while a remarkable new insight altered her relationship with her father, a practising Catholic priest.

Paperback: 978-1-78535-254-6 ebook: 978-1-78535-255-3

The Ecology of the Soul

A Manual of Peace, Power and Personal Growth for Real People in the Real World

Aidan Walker

Balance your own inner Ecology of the Soul to regain your natural state of peace, power and wellbeing.

Paperback: 978-1-78279-850-7 ebook: 978-1-78279-849-1

Not I, Not other than I

The Life and Teachings of Russel Williams

Steve Taylor, Russel Williams

The miraculous life and inspiring teachings of one of the World's greatest living Sages.

Paperback: 978-1-78279-729-6 ebook: 978-1-78279-728-9

On the Other Side of Love
A woman's unconventional journey towards wisdom
Muriel Maufroy
When life has lost all meaning, what do you do?
Paperback: 978-1-78535-281-2 ebook: 978-1-78535-282-9

Practicing A Course In Miracles
A translation of the Workbook in plain language, with mentor's notes
Elizabeth A. Cronkhite
The practical second and third volumes of The Plain-Language *A Course In Miracles*.
Paperback: 978-1-84694-403-1 ebook: 978-1-78099-072-9

Quantum Bliss
The Quantum Mechanics of Happiness, Abundance, and Health
George S. Mentz
Quantum Bliss is the breakthrough summary of success and spirituality secrets that customers have been waiting for.
Paperback: 978-1-78535-203-4 ebook: 978-1-78535-204-1

The Upside Down Mountain
Mags MacKean
A must-read for anyone weary of chasing success and happiness – one woman's inspirational journey swapping the uphill slog for the downhill slope.
Paperback: 978-1-78535-171-6 ebook: 978-1-78535-172-3

Your Personal Tuning Fork
The Endocrine System
Deborah Bates
Discover your body's health secret, the endocrine system, and 'twang' your way to sustainable health!
Paperback: 978-1-84694-503-8 ebook: 978-1-78099-697-4

Readers of ebooks can buy or view any of these bestsellers by clicking on the live link in the title. Most titles are published in paperback and as an ebook. Paperbacks are available in traditional bookshops. Both print and ebook formats are available online.
Find more titles and sign up to our readers' newsletter at http://www.johnhuntpublishing.com/mind-body-spirit
Follow us on Facebook at https://www.facebook.com/OBooks/ and Twitter at https://twitter.com/obooks